HAZING 101

HOW WE DID IT AND WHY WE DID IT

DARREN W. BRYCE

intension
INTENSION PUBLISHING

This book is available at special quantity discounts for bulk purchases for sales promotions, premiums, fund-raising, educational, or institutional use. Special book excerpts or customized printings can also be created to fit specific needs. For details, email Darren Bryce at Darren@collegelifeXtreme.com.

ISBN 1453646531

First Printing: June 2010
Printed in the United States of America by
Intension Publishing
www.intensionpublishing.com

Dedicated to the Brothers of Upsilon

We laughed

We fought

We loved

We hated

And we did it all for the good of the fraternity

CONTENTS

CHAPTERS

ACKNOWLEDGMENTS

I am grateful for having been born into a family that truly understands the meaning of unconditional love. Thank you for always supporting me through my many college years of self-discovery.

I am further indebted to The 706 Crew, The Younger Brothers, The Romans, and The Group. Every young man needs a tribe. I was fortunate enough to count myself a member of your collective associations.

Blake, Jeremy, Jeremy, Jason, Jason, Tiffany, and the many readers who suffered through earlier versions of this book. Thank you for the feedback and positive criticism. These stories reflect your invaluable input.

I would also like to thank Ian Coburn (God is a Woman: Dating Disasters), Tucker Max (Asshole Finish First; I Hope They Serve Beer in Hell), Maddox (The Alphabet of Manliness), Frank Kelly Rich (The Modern Drunkard), Neil Strauss (Emergency: This Book Will Save Your Life; The Game: Penetrating the Secret Society of Pickup Artists; Rules of the Game), Robert Hamburger (REAL Ultimate Power: The Official Ninja Book), Chuck Klosterman (Downtown Owl: A Novel; Sex, Drugs, and Cocoa Puffs: A Low Culture Manifesto), Chad Kultgen (The Lie; The Average American Male), Dick Masterson (Men Are Better Than Women), Tucker Max (I Hope they Serve Beer in Hell), Daniel Maurer (Brocabulary: The New Man-i-festo of Dude Talk), Justin Halpern (Shit My Dad Says), and all the other fratire writers who are proving that a market exists for politically incorrect literature. May they continue to spread the madness and release man from the chains of feminism.

AUTHOR'S NOTE

All names in this book are pseudonyms.

In some instances, I have taken the speech and behavior of any number of people and combined these characteristics into a composite person.

I have attributed specific quotes to people who undoubtedly did not say in real life exactly what they say in this book. I intend these quotes to be approximations, in subject matter and in tone, of what they actually said.

I have attributed specific actions and behaviors to people who undoubtedly did not do in real life what they do in this book.

I have time-compressed several sequences in this book and have periodically changed the locations of events I describe. I have also removed certain people from certain events.

Certain dates, actions, characteristics, and places have been changed to protect me from criminal prosecution and liability.

The names of fraternities and sororities in this book are fictional. Any similarity to real Greek organizations is purely coincidental.

The opinions and ideas expressed in this book are to be regarded as the property and creation of this author and are in no way affiliated with Florida State University, the City of Tallahassee, or any other institution.

Nevertheless, subject to these exceptions, this book is to the best of my ability an accurate accounting of the truth.

A character key has been added to the end of this book for your reading convenience.

FALL
Sophomore Year

CHAPTER ONE

FUCKING ALUMNI

"Throw me a frickin bone!"

"This is bullshit," the pledge said. "I can't believe they're making us do this every week."

"I know, dude," his roommate replied. "And that call-in we had Thursday night was brutal. What do you think Hell Week is gonna be like?"

"I heard they try to make us fuck a bull."

"Dude, I heard we have to do an elephant walk."

"A what?"

"An elephant walk. They make us line up and walk in a circle with our hand on the dick behind us and our thumb up the ass in front of us."

The pledge burst out laughing. "You're a moron for believing that shit. There's no way I'd ever do that."

"You'd fuck a bull?"

"Nah," he grinned, "maybe a cow. How was that Mu you fucked the other night? That bitch looked bovine as hell."

"Fuck you, dude. She still won't stop calling me."

The pledge chuckled. "Come on. Let's pick up the pace. We're gonna be late."

The pledge and his roommate started jogging across campus. They joined up with a few more Upsilon pledges who were all uniformly dressed in blue jeans and white t-shirts. It was 7:22 AM and they were heading to the Upsilon House for their Sunday morning work party. Most of the pledges looked dead tired because they had been drinking all night at a fraternity party.

"I think I'm gonna puke," Big Country groaned as they ran. "I didn't stop drinking until five o'clock this morning."

The pledge chuckled. "You look green as fuck. Must be those six keg stands you did."

"Seven," he corrected.

"Look, here comes Curtis," the pledge's roommate snickered. "That dumb shit wore a V-Neck."

Big Country laughed. "I bet Bryce gives him hell."

"Is *he* running things this morning?" the pledge asked.

"Yeah. He warned me not to be late."

"Bryce was still at the party when I left," said the pledge's roommate. "Maybe he won't even show up."

The pledge grinned. "And he probably went home and fucked Allison all morning. I know I would've."

"Hell yeah," his roommate agreed. "That girl's legs are ridiculous."

Big Country shook his head. "Bryce will be there. He's in ROTC, so he probably likes waking up early just to fucking haze us."

"Probably," the pledge grumbled. "I hope he doesn't bring Blake or Backstreet with him."

"I know, right? Those guys are mean as hell when they fucking haze."

But it wasn't Darren Bryce or his roommates who greeted the pledges when they arrived in the courtyard. It was Shultz and he was drunk as shit.

"Throw me a frickin bone!" Shultz yelled down at them from the rear building rooftop. "Throw me a frickin bone!"

The pledge stared up at the older brother with a grin. He liked and respected Shultz, something he couldn't say for several brothers he had already grown to despise. The 6ft 2 young man was a cool guy and was the best athlete in Upsilon. He had obviously been up all night drinking.

"Fuck you, pledges!" Shultz screamed. "Nice V-Neck, faggot!"

There were more than thirty pledges gathered in the fraternity house courtyard which looked like absolute shit.

Since it was a home game weekend, there were a lot of alumni in town and they always liked to break bottles and smash things up just so the pledges had something to clean.

"This place looks like ass," the pledge mumbled.

"Fucking alumni," his roommate said.

"Hey V-Neck!" Shultz yelled. "Drop down and give me twenty. NOW, BITCH!!!"

Curtis obliged and dropped to the concrete patio. The rest of the pledges sat on benches or pulled out smokes.

"What the fuck is wrong with you?" Darren Bryce suddenly screamed.

The shaved head, muscular young man entered the courtyard from the parking lot. He was dressed in black gym shorts and a black wife beater.

"If one of you does pushups, *all* of you do pushups!"

"Yeah!" Shultz yelled from the roof top. "Unity, bitches! Throw me a frickin bone!"

The drunk brother hurled a beer bottle over their heads which smashed against the front building of the fraternity house. Glass shattered and fell to the ground near the basement entrance—just more mess for them to clean up.

All of the young men dropped to the concrete and started doing push-ups.

The pledge was getting pissed. *What the fuck is wrong with these guys?* he silently asked. *It's 7:30 AM on a Sunday morning! I didn't join a fraternity to be a slave.*

"Alright, on your feet," Bryce said when they were finished. "Let's get this place cleaned up."

Dave emerged from his apartment and stood on the front building stairway. He stared down at the shattered bottle remains.

"What the hell, Shultz?" he yelled across the courtyard. "Are you throwing shit at my apartment?"

"The front of the house sucks!" Shultz chanted. "The front of the house sucks!"

Dave grabbed his cock and yelled, "Why don't you come suck this?"

"The front of the house sucks!" Shultz continued to shout. "The front of the house sucks!"

Before Dave could respond, his large roommate Santos came bursting out the door and launched two eggs over the courtyard at Shultz. His aim was poor and both projectiles fell short of their target.

"Nice throw, bitch!" Shultz screamed. "Try it again when you pull your panties out of your pussy lips."

"Fuck you," Santos mumbled. "I'm going back to sleep."

"The front of the house sucks!" Shultz chanted. "The front of the house sucks!"

The pledge and his pledge brothers watched this comical scene with amusement. This is why they had joined a fraternity, because they wanted to goof off and act out with cool brothers. *That and the pussy*, something the pledge's blue balls were aching for right now. He had brought home some random girl from the party last night who refused to take her jeans off when they were hooking up. She said she was a good girl, but maybe she was just a dirty girl with something to hide—like a pussy rash or an STD outbreak. The pledge shuddered at the thought.

"Hey, Bryce," Dave asked from the stairway, "have the pledges been practicing their song for the sorority houses?"

"Yup," Bryce answered. *"Bring it on Home to Me."*

Dave grinned. "You should take them into McMillan's room and serenade the girl he banged out last night."

Bryce laughed. "Who is she?"

"I don't know," he shrugged. "Some little Gamma ho."

"Good idea. Pledges, let's march."

Bryce led the entire pledge class into McMillan's tiny fraternity house bedroom where they proceeded to sing a full rendition of *Bring it on Home to Me*. McMillan laughed his ass off while the frat bunny hid under the covers in shame. The pledge caught a glimpse of her naked legs and noticed they were skinny. Too bad. It would have been funny as hell to catch the brother with a tons of fun fatty.

When they returned to the courtyard, Bryce assigned the cleanup duties.

"Goldman, I want you, Timmy, and Big Country to mop up the basement floor. Mike, I want you and Ray on toilets. Curtis, get the leaf blower and use that shit on the front deck. The rest of you find something else to do. I want this entire courtyard swept up and someone needs to vacuum the Formal Living Room and library."

They went to work, a small army of eighteen-year-old slaves cleaning up the filthy fraternity house. Some of the pledges were too lazy or too hungover to contribute, but most helped out because they knew the sooner the job got done, the sooner they could go the fuck home.

It took about an hour to clean the house. When they were finally finished, the pledges assembled in the courtyard and waited for Bryce to perform his inspection. Shultz was gone now. The pledge wondered if he had fallen off the roof and broken his neck. He hoped not. They needed Shultz for their IM football game against Epsilon this week,

"What's up, you fucking pledges?" asked a voice filled with bitterness.

An alumnus named Will entered the courtyard with a beer in his hand. The twenty-four year old graduated brother was a skinny little bitch with glasses and an attitude. He had been extremely drunk at the party last night where he acted like a dick to every pledge he saw.

"Into the basement," he said.

The pledges hesitated. Where was Bryce?

"Now goddamnit!" Will screamed.

The young men obeyed the command and scurried into the basement. Will walked in behind them. He sat on top of the DJ booth and stared at them menacingly.

"Lay on your backs right now," he said with a sneer.

They spread out and lay down on the bare basement floor. It smelled like soap from the recent mopping and it was still damp. The pledge felt his t-shirt soak up the moisture.

"Creed Speak," the alumnus said.

The pledges recited the Upsilon Creed which they were forced to memorize two weeks ago. Whenever a brother said the words "Creed Speak," they were required to say the entire creed out loud.

"Alphabet Speak," said the alumnus.

The pledges recited the Greek Alphabet they were also forced to memorize.

"Creed Speak."

They recited.

"Alphabet Speak."

They recited.

"Creed Speak."

They recited.

"Alphabet Speak."

They recited.

"Creed Speak."

Jesus Christ! The pledge screamed inside his head. *Are you gonna make us do this all day long? Don't you have anything better to do than screw with a bunch of eighteen-year-olds you've never met before this weekend and will probably never see again? Fucking tool!*

But another speak command did not follow. The alumnus with glasses sipped his beer and stared down at them with contempt.

"So I have a question for you pledges…how come none of you got my interview? I've been here all weekend long and not one of you asked for it."

All of the pledges were required to interview ten brothers every week. Getting interviews from alumni was worth double, but the pledge could think of a million reasons why none of them had asked for Will's interview. Maybe they didn't have their interview books when they saw him at the party last night. Or maybe they didn't have time to get interviews Saturday afternoon when they were too busy doing bitch work for brothers like fetching them beers. Maybe they were actually trying to have a good time with the girls who came by the fraternity house before and after the game. Or maybe they didn't want to get Will's interview because they thought he was a prick on a power trip who was probably somebody's bitch in the real world where he stared at a computer screen and crunched numbers for a company that saw him as nothing more than a number. There were plenty of reasons why they didn't get his interview, but none were any the pledge was willing to say out loud.

"Not one of you got my interview," Will continued. "Don't you little shits have any respect for alumni?"

How were they supposed to respond to that? Giving an answer would put you in the spot-light. It was better to stay quiet and be protected by the herd.

"Where's Smith at?" Will asked. "Smith, raise your fucking hand."

The pledge lifted his head up and saw Smith raise his hand. Smith was a cool kid who had allegedly left the party last night to bang out some hot little Delta slut.

Will slid off the DJ booth and walked towards his prey. He strolled right through the jigsaw puzzle of pledges lying on the ground, nudging them out of the way with his foot. It didn't hurt, not physically, but it pissed the pledge off.

Who the hell do you think you are? And why the fuck do you want to waste your time fucking with us? You're visiting a college town. Shouldn't you be having morning sex right now with some skanky college girl you met at the party? Fucking loser, you probably couldn't even pull ass when you were in college and last night's failure reminded you of this and now you're taking out your frustration on the only people in the world willing to put up with your shit—pledges.

The pledge hated fucking alumni and the pledge hated being a fucking pledge, but at least he wasn't Smith right now.

"What the hell is wrong with you?" Will screamed down in Smith's face. "I told you to get me a beer last night and you fucking disappeared!"

"I had to leave, dude," Smith foolishly replied. "Some girl wanted me to take her home."

"Fuck you, pledge! When alumni tell you to do something, you fucking do it!"

"I'm sorry, Sir."

"Yeah, you *are* sorry," Will said smugly and poured his beer on the kid's face. "If you don't want to bring *me* a beer, then I'll bring *you* one."

Smith violently coughed up the liquid that spilled into his mouth and nose. The alumnus laughed hideously, like the Dungeons and Dragons nerd he probably was in High School.

Seriously, the pledge thought, *what kind of four-eyed reject doesn't invest in contacts?*

"You guys fucking suck!" Will snarled and headed towards the door. "Creed Speak!"

When they finished reciting the Upsilon Creed, Bryce reappeared and was holding an axe. He stared down at them with a peculiar expression on his face. It almost looked like sympathy. Almost.

"Alright, boys," Bryce said, "stand up and follow me."

The pledges climbed to their feet and followed him towards the door. Bryce stopped when he saw the fresh puddle of beer on the ground.

"You guys just cleaned the house and now you're gonna leave that here? Show a little pride, gentlemen. This is *your* house too." His gaze shifted to Curtis. "Take that fucking V-Neck off and clean it up."

Curtis pulled his shirt off, crouched down, and wiped up the beer.

"Well done," Bryce said. "Let's go."

They followed him out the door, through the courtyard, and into the gravel parking lot. Cars and trucks were packed in like sardines. Quite a few brothers had passed out somewhere in the house last night instead of driving home. The pledge hoped the work party ended soon because he didn't want any of these brothers to wake up with hangovers and the cranky urge to haze pledges.

Bryce came to a halt in front of a very large oak. The tree was over a hundred feet high with the circumference of three telephone poles. There was a big gouge on the trunk where an axe had been swung many times.

"So tell me something," Bryce asked them. "How'd you guys like dealing with Will this morning?"

No one answered. It would have been sacrilege to speak poorly of alumni. Was Bryce testing them? Was he trying to trick them into saying something they shouldn't just so he'd have an excuse to haze them?

Bryce chuckled. "Fine. I'll say what you guys can't. Will is a little bitch. Instead of fucking with you guys this morning, he should be fucking some slut he went home with last night, but he didn't hook up, so he's pissed."

The young men laughed and the pledge smiled because he had drawn the very same conclusion about Will. Bryce could be a mean motherfucker when he wanted to be, but he definitely had a cool side to him.

"Dealing with guys like Will sucks," Bryce said, "but it goes with the territory. When you're a pledge, you get hazed by brothers you don't like. Someday you'll be hazing pledges that don't like you. That's the system, gentlemen. And it's never gonna change."

The pledge knew Bryce was right. Sometimes he forgot that the guys who hazed him went through the exact same shit. And sometimes he forgot how much fun it was gonna be when he was the finally the one hazing.

Still, thought the pledge, *that doesn't mean we deserve to be hazed by a fucking loser like Will. There ought to be some sort of minimum qualifications to haze pledges, like you have to be able to bench press 250 pounds or you have to be able to pull hot bitches. No one should have to be hazed by someone they don't respect and how do you respect a pussy who can't get pussy?*

"It's not gonna change," Bryce continued, "but that doesn't mean you have to like it. That doesn't mean you can't hate it."

The pledge did hate it. All of them did.

"I know you guys are pissed and I don't want you leaving here hating Upsilon, so we're gonna do a little Anger Management 101 right now."

The pledge stared at the axe and the oak tree with old chopping marks on it. This could be interesting.

Bryce nodded. "I'm gonna give each of you a turn on my tree. I want you to swing this axe like your swinging it at Will. Think about lying on your backs on a Sunday fucking morning, putting up with his crap. Think about how that made you feel and then let that shit all out."

The pledge smiled. Was this something other pledge classes had done or was this Bryce's personal anger management system?

"Here ya go, meat," Bryce said to Curtis. "Show me something."

The shirtless young man took the axe and stared at it uncertainly. Curtis had a decent build, but he didn't look like the type of guy who enjoyed mayhem and destruction.

"Just hit the tree?" he asked.

"No, don't hit it," Blake replied. "Chop that bitch, motherfucker."

Curtis took a step forward and hesitantly swung the axe against the oak tree.

"Like that?" he asked.

"Again," Bryce answered. "But this time rage on that thing like you mean it and don't fucking stop until you feel like you've killed someone."

Curtis nodded and swung the axe for ten solid strikes, but Bryce was still not impressed.

"Weak," he said. "Fucking weak. Someone better show me some fucking anger."

Goldman stepped up and he too failed to impress Bryce with his timid axe swinging.

The pledge was not surprised by Goldman's dismal performance. He was a pussy. Everybody knew that. In fact, the pledge asked himself at least twice a day why he was willing to join a fraternity that let a guy like Goldman pledge.

"Give me that fucking thing!" Bryce snarled and grabbed the axe from Goldman. "Let me show you bitches what I'm talking about!"

He stepped closer to the tree and held the axe in his hands like he was preparing for combat.

"Do you think I liked being hazed when I was a pledge? Do you think I'm the kind of guy to take shit from anyone?"

The pledge stared at the shaved head, muscular young man whose nostrils flared with anger. Bryce was definitely not a pushover.

"Do you know how I made it through Hell Week when I was a pledge? I fucking chopped trees downs! If a brother hazed me, I chopped a tree down. If a brother fucked with me, I chopped a tree down!"

He was swinging the axe now. Brutally. The dull blade struck the oak tree with tremendous force and splinters of wood fell to the ground

"Chopped a fucking tree!" Bryce screamed as if he was reliving his days of pledgehood. "Chopped a fucking tree!"

He attacked the tree like he was savagely hacking up a human body on the battlefield. When he was finished, he threw the axe to the ground, spit on the tree, and kicked it.

"Fuck this tree!" Bryce cursed. "Fuck this tree and fuck

being hazed! That's the kind of intensity I want to see from you guys! Show me some goddamn hatred!"

The pledges were taken aback by this. How could anyone muster that kind of rage at 8:30 in the morning on a Sunday? Bryce definitely had some issues, but his performance stirred their blood.

The pledge picked up the axe and started swinging it madly against the tree as if Will really was standing before him. He hated Will. He hated being hazed. He hated that fucking tree.

"Fuck you!" he cursed as he chopped. "Fuck you, you fucking bitch alumni!"

Bryce smiled.

When the pledge was done, he kicked the tree and handed the axe to a large pledge named Raul. The Latino took the instrument and also went to town on the tree, striking it with crazed fury.

Next up was Big Country. He still looked incredibly hungover, but the stout young man swung the axe with impressive strength.

"Come on, Big Country!" Bryce egged him on. "Is that all you got!"

The buzz cut freshman swung the axe even harder.

"Come on!" Bryce screamed. "Show me how you do it back on the farm when you're chopping up firewood and shit! Think about Will hazing you!"

Big Country's faced began to change as he swung the axe. Weariness became determination and determination became rage. He no longer cared about how he felt, what he looked like, or who had pissed him off. Hatred consumed him and all he cared about was killing that fucking tree.

Bryce saw all this and he smiled. "Good. Very fucking good. Who's next?"

Big Country handed the axe off to Smith. Five seconds later he was puking behind a truck. When Bryce walked around the vehicle and saw the pledge vomiting, he laughed his ass off.

"That's fucking outstanding," Bryce said. "I'm definitely taking you as my little brother this semester."

Big Country smiled and puked some more.

CHAPTER TWO

THE CONSPIRACY

"For the good of the fraternity."

"I'm telling you guys," I said, "Friday night was fucking ridiculous. LATE NIGHT was rented out by the Alphas and two other fraternities and it was packed with the best-looking sorority girls on campus."

"There was some hot bitches there, huh?" Blake asked.

"Hell yeah. I've never seen that many hot girls in one place, looking for cock. We're definitely getting ripped off by our Greek experience."

Backstreet was lying sideways on the loveseat with his hands clasped behind his head and his legs hanging over the armrest. He turned towards me and nodded.

"I know what you mean," he said. "I think the same shit every time COURSE 701 gets rented out for date socials by the top sororities and I have to pour drinks for all those girls dressed up in slutty little costumes. We're getting jipped."

I stared at my roommate and asked, "Why'd you join a fraternity, Backstreet? I never considered myself to be the kind of guy to join a fraternity, but I decided to check out Rush Week because my cousin at K-State swore to me that fraternity guys fuck the hottest girls on campus."

"That's why I joined too. I remember talking to guys in the gym who told me that fraternity guys get all the pussy. But not just pussy—*sorority* pussy."

"And what has Upsilon provided?" I asked cynically.

Blake was sitting next to me on the couch. He snorted and answered, "Socials with fat girl sororities."

I nodded. "Every now and then we get a decent sorority, but usually we get stuck with the lower tier. Shit! We had to do Homecoming this year with the fucking Mus!"

"Hell yeah," Blake said. "Fuck those big bone bitches."

Backstreet shook his head in frustration. "The only time we even interact with the top sororities is when we go to their houses and serenade them with the pledges. *It's bullshit.*"

"Complete bullshit," I agreed. "I'm tired of paying dues to belong to a fraternity that prevents me from getting laid more than it helps me. And I'm tired of girls thinking less of us when they see kids at our parties like goofy ass Glenn and Pete with his lopsided head."

Blake snorted. "Fuck girls seeing them! *I'm* tired of seeing those motherfuckers hanging around."

"Hell yeah," I chuckled. "If *we* don't want to be around those guys, then why the hell would any hot sorority girl want to be near them?"

Backstreet stood up and walked into the kitchen to make a protein shake. When the sound of the blender ceased, he returned to the living room with a plastic cup in hand.

"You know," he said thoughtfully, "every time we meet new girls and bring them by the fraternity, they really do think less of us." He sipped the protein shake and shrugged. "But this shit has been going on for years, even before we got here. Kids that don't bring anything positive to the fraternity are always allowed to slide through."

"At least we got that fucking kid Dickey out," Blake offered optimistically.

I shook my head in disagreement. "But look at how many kids we *didn't* get blackballed. Look at what happened with Dexter. We tried to get him kicked out when we were pledges and our self-righteous older brothers hazed us for it because they said it wasn't an act of unity."

"That was stupid as hell," Backstreet said with a flick of his tongue ring. "The whole fucking point of unity is to unite with guys who make you stronger, not guys who make you weaker."

16

Blake hissed in irritation. "The older brothers don't know shit about building a good fraternity. All we ever do is repeat the same mistakes over and over again."

"It's fucking bullshit," I said. "We got pledges right now that should be blackballed, but no one's gonna do it."

"Like who?" Backstreet asked. "Goldman?"

"Goldman, Pebbles, and Timmy," I declared in a voice thick with disdain.

"Yeah," Blake agreed. "*All* those kids need to go."

Backstreet nodded his head slowly. "Guys like that don't contribute shit to our fraternity. Fuck that, they're actually making a negative contribution."

The room went silent for a few moments. Our eyes followed a football game on television, but our minds were assessing the many shortcomings of our brotherhood.

Shaking my head in frustration, I finally asked, "I guess the real question is, why'd you guys join Upsilon instead of a better fraternity?"

"Diversity," Blake instantly replied.

"Yup," Backstreet agreed. "Diversity. Because we're not a bunch of clones like the Alphas or Epsilon."

I nodded. "I think diversity is a good thing too, but only when it's a diversity of type, not quality."

"What do you mean?" Backstreet asked.

"I mean I wouldn't want to belong to a fraternity where everyone talks the same, dresses the same, or acts the same, but I *do* want to belong to a fraternity that requires every brother to pull ass or kick ass."

"Hell yeah, yo," Blake said. "You gotta bring something to the table."

I nodded. "Being different doesn't give someone quality, quality gives them quality. A stud is a stud no matter what side of the tracks he's from."

Backstreet chuckled. "And a tool is a tool no matter what side of the tracks he's from."

"Exactly. Goldman, Pebbles, and Timmy are different from us because they lack social quality. That's not good diversity. That's just weakness."

"But what do we do about it now?" Blake asked. "The older brothers will never let us get rid of those kids. They're all about *quantity*, not quality."

Backstreet sneered. "The only reason they want a big pledge class is because we need all the new member dues because so many older brothers aren't paying *their* dues."

"Nah, yo," Blake said with a short laugh. "The only reason the older brothers want to keep loser pledges around is because they're losers too and they're looking out for their own."

Backstreet laughed, but the validity of Blake's words increased my frustration. I sat up on the couch and flicked off the television with the remote control. Enough was enough. I was tired of complaining about my fraternity and doing nothing about it. Talk was cheap. It was time to take action.

"I'm fucking sick of this shit," I said. "And I'm sick of the older brothers calling the shots. Let's have a meeting. We'll get all the younger brothers over here we can trust and we'll organize a voting block to blackball these kids tonight."

Backstreet's eyes widened with excitement. "We got the numbers. There's definitely enough of us who want those three pledges gone."

"Let's do it," Blake replied with a malicious smile. "Yo, this will be controversial as hell. I fucking love shit like that!"

Less than an hour later, the twenty younger brothers we invited to our secret meeting began to arrive. I had already dragged the dining table to the far end of the living room and placed two chairs behind it. Backstreet and I sat in these chairs, intending to orchestrate things like a mock Chapter meeting. Brothers slowly trickled into the apartment and sat on couches, chairs, and the floor. When the last group had arrived, we locked the door and initiated the younger brother conspiracy.

"Gentlemen," I said and waited for silence to fall on the room. "We've called this meeting to discuss the pledges. Most of you have gotten to know them by now."

"Yeah," someone grumbled. "They all fucking suck."

The room full of brothers broke out with laughter.

"Some of them *do* suck," I continued, "and that's why we've called you here today. It's our contention that Goldman, Timmy, and Pebbles will not make a positive contribution to Upsilon."

Backstreet spoke next. "We want to call a voting box on the pledges during Chapter. Do any of you guys want to blackball these three pledges?"

"Hell the fuck yeah," Mitchell immediately replied. "Let's get rid of them tonight."

His roommate Fish nodded. "Yeah, I'll vote them out."

"Blackball those motherfuckers!" Mendez exclaimed. "They're all worthless and Goldman is the biggest tool I've ever met in my life."

Other brothers started launching criticism.

"Those kids are terrible!"

"Blackball them tonight."

"I'll vote them out twice."

A young man named Rocks giggled and said, "Did you see Goldman take his shirt off the other day? He's got cellulite all over his stomach."

Blake snorted. "Yo, he used to be a fat kid in High School. That's not cellulite. It's stretch marks and loose skin."

"What about Timmy?" Moody cried out. "That short little shit looks like an educated Keebler Elf with those thick-rimmed glasses he's been wearing."

The room erupted with laughter.

"What about Pebbles?" someone asked.

"Pebbles needs to go too," someone answered.

"Who the fuck is Pebbles?" Rowdy asked.

Blake chuckled. "That stocky kid with dirty-blonde hair and a bowling ball face."

"His real name is Keith," someone offered.

"Why do you guys call him Pebbles?" Rowdy asked.

Mitchell laughed. "Because he's the only person I've ever met dumber than Rocks."

Everyone looked at Rocks whose face flushed crimson. He looked daggers at Mitchell and cursed, "Fuck you, Mitchell!"

We all laughed. Rocks had earned his nickname because someone had once accused him of being as dumb as a pile of rocks.

"Pebbles needs to be blackballed." Rowdy said. "That pudgy kid doesn't have any personality or leadership ability."

"And he definitely doesn't pull bitches," Mendez said.

"None of them do," I declared. "And that's the whole point. They aren't making a contribution to our brotherhood and they make us all look bad. It's an ugly truth, gentlemen. But it's the reality we face."

A tall, red-haired brother named Jacob stood up from his chair. The brazen young man was renowned for speaking his mind. He was also infamous for being a drunk, a reputation that seemed validated by the twelve pack of Natty-Light at his feet.

"I'm tired of letting guys in here that don't contribute. We need leaders. We need athletes. And we definitely need some more face guys around here."

The assembly of brothers grunted in agreement and a score of other criticisms were put forth, some real, some in jest. But the bottom line was that the three pledges were weak, unpopular, and unattractive, and had we not been in a fraternity with these individuals, the young men sitting in my living room would never have associated with them on a social level. It was therefore not a very long or divisive debate. We all believed we deserved better than Upsilon was providing and we were eager for change.

"So who's gonna call the box session?" Moody asked.

The excited chatter came to an end and brothers stared at each other in silence. Blackballing brothers was always a controversial issue and no one ever wanted to be the asshole to call the box session at Chapter. I know I didn't.

"Fuck it," Backstreet suddenly said. "I'll do it. I'll call the boxes if you guys back me up with your blackball votes."

"You got my vote," Mendez offered.

"Definitely," Mitchell agreed.

"These kids are history," Jacob said. "We're a hundred percent behind you."

"Hell yeah," Blake said, eyeing Backstreet with more respect than I had ever seen him show our roommate. "You're the fucking man."

I nodded. "Good. Thank you, Backstreet. If the brothers in this room vote according to plan, then we'll have all the votes we need."

"If they vote according to plan," Moody mumbled cynically.

This statement caused Cortez to stand up from where he was sitting on the carpet. The handsome Latino from Miami was an athletically-built young man with a rightfully earned badass reputation. Cortez rarely spoke up at our Chapter meetings, but this was not due to any shyness on his part. Cortez was the kind of guy who took the time to choose his words wisely, and when he spoke, people always listened.

"This meeting is long overdue," he said. "I've never regretted my decision to join Upsilon. I've had some great times here and I've made some of the best friends I've ever had, but things *do* need to change."

His penetrating dark eyes darted around the room and he continued, "I know all you guys feel it too, bro. I know you want to make this place better. But there's a lot of talk around here, good ideas that nobody every follows through with."

Cortez paused for a moment to let his words sink in, and when he spoke again, his voice was filled with conviction.

"Tonight, I say we follow through. Let's get rid of these kids none of us would be hanging out with if they weren't in our fraternity."

Brothers snapped their fingers in approval and Blake stood up from the couch.

"Cortez is right," he said. "I'm tired of people not following through around here. We've tried to blackball kids before, and then when it comes time to vote, people always bitch out. That's not gonna happen tonight. Tonight we do it for the good of the fraternity."

"For the good of the fraternity," I repeated.

"For the good of the fraternity," echoed the room of brothers.

CHAPTER THREE

BLACKBALLED

"Fuck that! Tell him to fucking leave!"

Less than an hour later, I was sitting in the basement of the Upsilon fraternity house as our Chapter meeting went through its standard protocol. We stood together as a brotherhood and recited our creed in unison. The IFC rep reported the information he received from his weekly meeting with the Inter-Fraternity Council. Our social chairman discussed an upcoming *Bikers and Babes* date social. The intramural sports chairman informed us that we had slipped into third place behind the Alphas and the Omicrons in the campus intramural rankings because of our poorer than usual performance in flag football.

Towards the end of Chapter, the seriousness of the meeting would always fade and antsy brothers unable to sit still longer than an hour would start acting up and cracking jokes. Like clockwork, I watched the older brothers loosen up as the meeting appeared to be coming to an end, or so they thought. When it came time for general announcements, Backstreet stood up and dropped the bomb.

"I want to do a box session for the pledges," he said.

The effect of his words was instant pandemonium.

"What the hell for?"

"They're almost brothers!"

"Hell week is two weeks away!"

"Are you fucking serious?"

Most of the older brothers were in an uproar and a few of the younger brothers were equally incensed. Since the pledges were so close to being initiated, some brothers felt that it was unethical to call a box session on them at this late juncture. Others thought that if a pledge was really a problem, he would have already been blackballed. A few brothers even rationalized that because the pledges had made it this far, they had proven they wanted to be a part of our fraternity and this was all that mattered.

"Fuck that!" Moody yelled as he jumped to his feet. "We're brothers of this fraternity and it's our right to call a box on any pledge we want at any time we want!"

His voice was seconded by many other younger brothers who had been present at the secret meeting. We would have our day, and no one would take it from us, not even the older brothers.

Arguments continued to flare until Mitchell, the Sergeant-at-Arms, threatened to kick brothers out of the basement if they did not settle down. With much regret, the Pledge Marshall began to read off the names of our pledges.

"Greg Goldman," he said first.

Backstreet immediately stood up and said, "Box."

The angry look on the faces of the older brothers was priceless, but it was nowhere near as hilarious as the enraged expressions that formed on their faces when the names of Timmy and Pebbles were called. Once again, Backstreet was the voice of instigation.

He stood up each time and said, "Yeah…uh…this is another guy I want to call a box on."

Pandemonium.

"What the fuck, Backstreet?"

"Do you want to kick them all out?"

"We need the fucking dues!"

"How can you dick someone over like that?"

"They're almost brothers!"

"How can you do that? Do you even care about their feelings?"

As more brothers cursed and shouted, I stared at my blonde-haired roommate with admiration. It was not an easy thing to place someone on the chopping block, but Backstreet proved himself to be a young man willing to put the interests of his brotherhood before all else.

When the entire list of pledges had been read, a separate hand vote was conducted for each of the three pledges under review, and much to my disappointment, Goldman was the only pledge who accumulated enough blackball votes to be kicked out of the fraternity. Many of the older brothers were still appalled by this outcome.

A brainiac brother named Preston stood up and stormed out of the basement, but not before turning around and bitterly exclaiming, "Since you assholes want him out, then you guys are the ones who are gonna tell him to his face he's been blackballed!"

"No problem," Mitchell replied as he stood to his feet and followed Preston out the door.

I watched them leave with amusement and respect. Mitchell was in his element now. The young man was a criminology major who wanted to be a cop, something I knew my friend would be quite good at because he had no problem telling people what they didn't want to hear. Mitchell was terrific at being a dick.

When Mitchell left the basement, he walked around the rear building of the fraternity house to where all of the pledges were waiting for Chapter to end and their Sunday meeting to begin.

"Hey, Goldman," Mitchell said as he approached the gathered pledges, "you need to come with me."

The pledge followed him through the courtyard, up the back stairway, into the fraternity house, and out the front door. By the time they crossed Pensacola Street, the young pledge had a sense of what was happening.

"Here," Mitchell suggested, "let's sit down."

They sat on a short flight of steps leading up to a faculty parking lot. With as much gentleness as possible,

Mitchell initiated what would be the most traumatizing event to have ever occurred in the pledge's young life.

"Goldman, you've been blackballed from Upsilon."

The young man stared blankly at Mitchell. He heard the brother's words, but he couldn't quite believe them.

"This doesn't mean you have to stop being friends with your pledge brothers or anyone else in the fraternity, but what it does mean is that you won't ever wear our letters on campus and you can't come to our fraternity sponsored events."

Goldman's red-haired head sunk low in agony and Mitchell could almost hear the pledge's heart breaking. When Goldman looked up again, there were tears in his blue eyes.

"Mitchell," he whispered, "you don't know what this place means to me. I…I consider you guys my friends. I know that you, Bryce, and some of the other brothers don't like me…but I want you guys to know that I have nothing against you. I just want to be a part of this fraternity."

Mitchell voice became sterner. "I'm sorry, Goldman, but this is just not the right place for you."

This statement was met with an awkward silence, interrupted only by the noise of cars whizzing by on Pensacola Street and the quivering sound of the young pledge sniffling. Refusing to feel pity for the heartbroken freshman, Mitchell tried to give the young man a gentle push in the direction of pride.

"Look, bro," he said, "if I were in your shoes, I'd be like, 'Fuck these guys,' and just walk away and not look back."

But Goldman did not have enough pride to walk away, and instead of holding fast to what dignity he had left, the young man started to beg.

"Please, Mitchell," he pleaded, "just tell me what I need to do to stay here…I swear I'll do whatever it takes…I'll do *whatever* it takes."

The sad and desperate way Goldman was looking at

Mitchell made him feel like he was taking a cow out of the barn to be slaughtered, but he raised the shotgun to the animal's head and fired.

"I'm sorry, Goldman. It's out of my hands. You've been blackballed. The fraternity has spoken."

The brother of Upsilon rose to his feet and left the crying freshman on the stairs. Goldman's morose reaction to the bad news should not have been a surprise to anyone who knew him personally and knew of his dependency on the fraternity for a social life. While most guys would certainly have been grieved and humiliated by the whole ordeal, they would also have been resentful enough to move on with their lives. But Goldman needed the fraternity for the social life he would never be able to build on his own which was precisely why he was not the type of guy we wanted in Upsilon.

A few minutes after Mitchell returned to the fraternity house, the anguished freshman walked around the side of the building and entered the courtyard. Brothers and pledges watched him with mixed emotions.

"They just blackballed me, guys!" Goldman cried to his pledge brothers. "They fucking blackballed me."

"I'm sorry, Goldman," a pledge said and looked like he meant it.

"Yeah, dude…we're sorry," said another pledge who looked like he didn't.

Goldman approached a group of older brothers and I moved closer to listen.

"Bishop?" he whimpered. "What'd I do wrong? I thought you liked me."

"I do like you," Bishop said and gently laid his hand on the other young man's shoulder. "And you didn't do anything wrong."

"Then what's wrong with *me?*" Goldman asked, terrified of what the answer might be.

"There's nothing wrong with you!" Preston urged as he

stared venomously at me and the younger brothers. "You're a good kid and any fraternity should be glad to have you."

"Then why...why, guys?" he asked.

"It was bullshit," answered an older brother named Lewis. "It was fucking bullshit."

"I'm sorry, Goldman," Bishop said. "I don't agree with it, but sometimes these things happen."

I too did my part to console the kid. "Don't worry, Goldman. We can give you your money back."

Goldman's reaction to this backhanded insult was to shake his head and cry even harder.

Preston looked at me in horrified disgust. "That's the *last* thing he's concerned with right now!"

It was not my intention to increase Goldman's pain, but I realized it was a rotten thing to say. Regrettably, Mitchell and I would not be the only brothers to cause Goldman grief. When Backstreet saw the pledge in the courtyard, he was beyond furious.

"What the fuck is Goldman still doing here?" he yelled.

"Relax, Backstreet," Mitchell said and stared at his fraternity brother in shock. "The kid is just saying goodbye to his friends."

"Fuck that! Tell him to leave right fucking now!"

Goldman flinched at these harsh words. It was cold thing to say to the freshman, but it was also a necessary thing to say. Goldman was like a stray dog that had been fed one too many times. If he was not subjected to open rebuke and hostility, he would have kept coming around to seek the company of people who did not really want him for a pet.

The devastated young man left the fraternity house and walked back to his dormitory alone, ashamed, and broken.

Most of the brothers who voted to blackball the pledge felt some degree of guilt or pity. It was hard not to feel sympathy for a guy who was crying because he so desperately wanted to be a part of your organization. But deeper than this empathy for Goldman there simmered within our hearts a fire of joy that was our finest hour as brothers of Upsilon. We grinned like excited children and gave each other handshakes and pats on the back. It truly felt like we had finally taken a huge step in the right direction to improve the reputation of our fraternity.

My roommates and I watched the scene of excited younger brothers with a gloating feeling of satisfaction.

"That was awesome," Blake said.

"Hell yeah, it was," I agreed. "This is the turning point."

"You think?"

"Absolutely," Backstreet said. "Goldman is just one kid, but blackballing him is a symbol of the new way things are gonna be from now on."

I nodded and sagely proclaimed, *"The old guard has lost its first crucial battle to the next generation of Upsilon brothers who will restore the fraternity to its former greatness."*

Blake chuckled. "Hell yeah, yo. Too bad we couldn't get rid of all three of them."

We stared at Pebbles and Timmy as they followed their pledge brothers into the basement for their Sunday meeting. As the Assistant Pledge Marshall, I was supposed to be in there too, but I wanted to savor this moment for as long as possible.

"Hell Week." I said. "We'll get rid of them then."

Backstreet nodded as he fired up a Marlboro Light cigarette. I noticed Blake was watching our roommate with newfound respect in his eyes.

"You stepped up tonight," he said to Backstreet.

The short meathead shrugged and replied, "I did what had to be done.

"Nah, yo," Blake giggled, "you went beyond the call of duty. You were boxing kids left and right!"

"You are definitely the Box Master," I said with a grin.

Blake giggled again. "Don't fuck with Backstreet. He'll throw anybody out of here!"

Backstreet exhaled a cloud of smoke and spoke his next words with conviction. "If they don't contribute, they're fucking gone."

"Mitchell stepped up too," Blake said.

"Yeah, he did," I replied. "Telling Goldman to his face like that....I don't think I could've been the one to do it."

Blake looked at me and laughed. "You're the one who started all this shit."

"Yeah, I know...but I don't hate the kid. I don't even really dislike him. I just don't want him in my fraternity."

Blake shook his head. "Nah, I hate that motherfucker."

I burst out laughing and stared at a group of older brothers who were quietly conferring about the blackballing of Goldman. It was certain they did not share our merry sentiment.

"Mitchell said Goldman starting begging," Blake said.

"You mean Officer Mitchell?" I asked.

"Tah ha," Blake giggled. "That motherfucker is gonna make one hell of a dickhead cop."

"Where'd he go, anyways?" I asked.

"Beats me."

"Over there," Backstreet said. "Heading towards the parking lot."

"I'll be back," I said. "I'm gonna go thank him."

I followed Mitchell down the stairs and into the parking lot. When I approached him, he was sitting behind the wheel of his red truck with a strange look on his face. Extending my hand through the window, I attempted to reassure him.

"It *had* to be done," I said. "This is not the right place for him. You did a good thing tonight."

Mitchell shook my hand. "Bro, it was ugly. The kid started begging."

"Are you surprised?"

"Yeah…a little. I knew he'd cry like a bitch, but I didn't think he'd beg."

"That must've made you feel like shit."

"Nah," Mitchell replied as he absently rubbed his goatee. "To be honest, I kind of liked doing it."

I snorted. "You liked crushing his dreams?"

"No. I like living ours. We did it, Bryce."

"Yeah," I replied with an excited grin, "we did it."

CHAPTER FOUR

BROTHERLY RIVALRY

"Get used to it."

Later that evening when the exhilaration of our victory was still simmering, my roommates and I sat in front of the television. We were watching *Braveheart* for the thousandth time and Blake was reciting the movie word for word. When we were freshmen, my roommate would get extremely wasted, stand up on his bed, and start making battle speeches like he was William Wallace. It was a hilarious sight to behold the short, muscular Honduran slur out animated gibberish about freedom and war with a cockeyed, drunk look in his eyes.

"Yo," I said, interrupting my roommate's line recitation, "I got interviewed yesterday by a few of the pledges. When they asked me what my favorite day in Upsilon was, I told them Desperado."

"*Desperado*," Blake sang musically. "Hell yeah. I love that shit."

"If they asked me the same question today, I'd give a different answer—the day we kicked Goldman out of the fraternity."

My roommates burst out laughing. "Me too," Backstreet agreed. "Today really was my best day in Upsilon."

"Hell yeah, yo." Blake said. "Fuck Goldman."

Backstreet's cell phone rang a few minutes later and he picked it up from the coffee table. My eyes remain fixated on the television and the sight of Mel Gibson decapitating an English lord.

"That shit was fucking brutal!" I exclaimed. "Play that back in slow motion."

Blake aimed the remote at the DVD player and was

about to replay the violent scene when Backstreet suddenly screamed, "Fuck that! They can't fucking do that shit!"

I glanced towards my blonde-haired roommate and saw a murderous look in his eyes. His face looked like it always looked right before he and Blake got into a fight.

"Hell no!" he yelled into the phone. "I'm not coming for that shit. He's blackballed! They can't bring him back!"

Blake and I stared at each other. *No fucking way.*

"Damn those assholes!" Backstreet snarled as he flung his cell phone to the carpet floor. "This is bullshit!"

"What happened?" Blake asked.

"There's gonna be a revote in one hour. Our fucking noble president Bishop and our fucking vice-president Lewis went digging through the bylaw manual looking for a loophole to save Goldman. They found one."

"Fucking older brothers," Blake cursed.

"Nah, man," I said. "This is Bishop. This is *all* Bishop."

"What do you mean?"

"After Goldman got blackballed tonight, Bishop took me aside all sad-like and shit and told me he felt guilty as hell about what happened."

"All those fuckers did," Blake grumbled.

"Yeah, but Bishop said that when Goldman's father was in town for Parents' weekend, he gave Bishop his business card and said to give him a call if he ever needed anything."

Backstreet asked, "So what...Bishop feels like he owes him or something?"

I nodded. "Exactly. The guy hates blackballing pledges and this made it a lot worse for him."

"Fuck Bishop!" Blake snarled. "I'll quit this fraternity before I let Goldman back in!"

Backstreet shook his head and said, "I can't believe these assholes are gonna try to save this kid on a fucking technicality!"

We called our friends involved with the organized movement to blackball Goldman. They were furious, but all agreed to return with us to the fraternity house to advance the younger brother political agenda.

When my roommates and I arrived, we marched straight to Bishop's apartment to see with our own eyes the bylaw justification for having a revote. I knocked loudly on the front door and Bishop answered a few seconds later.

"Hey, guys," he said timidly. "Come on in."

The President of Upsilon was a well-mannered individual of medium height and build. He had brown eyes and dark brown hair worn in a short, conservative hair-cut. Bishop always seemed to have the facial hair of a five o'clock shadow, but he was an attractive young man who might have been popular with the ladies if it were not for his complete deficiency of the aggressive cockiness so often possessed by alpha males. Bishop was a natural pacifist.

My roommates and I entered the apartment and saw Lewis sitting on the couch. He looked up at us with contempt and offered no greeting.

"We want to see it," Backstreet said abruptly.

"Yeah, let me see that shit," Bake snarled.

Bishop seemed intimidated by their demeanor, but he stuck his ground, pulled out the Upsilon bylaw manual, and pointed at the clause of contention.

"Take a look at this," he said. "We've been doing it wrong. One-third of the required quorum of sixty brothers is not enough to blackball pledges if six weeks of the pledge semester has passed. You need half the required quorum."

"So what?" I asked dismissively. "We've been doing it our own way for years and now all of a sudden we're gonna change things up for *Goldman*?"

"Yes," Lewis answered snidely from the couch.

Our vice-president was a short-little-man endowed with handsome enough features to win him a pretty girlfriend in the Theta sorority. Until that moment, I had always thought highly of him as a fraternity brother, but now I wanted to crush the midget's larynx with my foot.

Ignoring Lewis, I continued to stare down Bishop and challenge his executive decision.

"What about all the other pledges that have been blackballed over the years? Is this fair to them? Did the President of Upsilon go digging through the bylaws to save them because their daddies gave him a business card?"

"That's not what happened," Bishop urged. "I—"

"You're out of line doing this," Backstreet said, cutting him off. "This pledge should be tried and hanged by the same set of laws the rest of us have dealt with!"

"I understand you guys are upset," Bishop replied, "but there's a right and wrong way to handle these things and it's spelled out in this manual."

Lewis nodded. "That's why we're gonna have a revote, so we can do this thing the *right* way."

"Fuck a revote," Blake snarled. "That kid is fucking blackballed."

Backstreet flicked his tongue ring at the older brothers and said, "This is bullshit. The only reason you want a revote is because you didn't like what happened the first time!"

"I'm sorry you guys feel that way," Bishop said with false empathy. "But we have to abide by the rules and regulations of our fraternity."

My roommates and I left the apartment in disgust. Time and time again these fucking older brothers were standing in the way of progress. Why did they want to prevent something from happening that would ultimately make all of our social lives better? Why were they so fearful of change?

Out in the courtyard, over ninety brothers had amassed in anticipation of the revote. This was a much larger gathering than the sixty brothers who showed up earlier in the night for Chapter. Dispersed in small groups, the brothers were smoking cigarettes and heatedly discussing what was quickly becoming a controversy. Most of the older brothers were gathered to one side of the courtyard and the younger brothers stood together on the opposite side.

My roommates and I approached McMillan, Dave, and Borelli who seemed to be standing literally and metaphorically in-between the two warring factions. These three guys were all sociable, good-looking, athletic older brothers who I had always looked up to and respected.

"Borelli," I asked, "what the fuck is this shit? We blackball this kid and now you guys want to bring him back?"

The short, muscular Italian shook his head. "I don't want the kid around either, but bylaws are bylaws. We can't just kick a kid out without following the rules."

Blake's face curled with displeasure. "Yo, how the fuck are we supposed to follow the rules when they change whenever someone like Bishop doesn't like the results?"

I looked to Dave for support. Surely a stud like him would recognize the necessity of blackballing Goldman. But the handsome older brother shrugged his shoulders meekly.

"It's out of our hands," he said. "We don't have a choice."

"McMillan?" I asked, turning my eyes to the blonde-haired, hulking figure. "What the hell, man?"

"It sucks, I know," he replied and exhaled smoke from a cigarette. "But this is how things are done around here. Get used to it."

I shook my head in frustration. McMillan's apathy was almost excusable because he was up his girlfriend's ass this semester and no longer cared about what happened to the fraternity. But Dave and Borelli were two brothers who lived in the Upsilon House. A passive attitude was not what I expected from two respected brothers who should have been willing to challenge Bishop and his cronies. More than anything else, this was the real problem within my fraternity—

the right guys refused to lead.

My roommates and I left the trio and joined Mitchell, Klein, and Moody who were quietly conferring with a few other younger brothers no less revolted than we were by the political swindle of the older brothers.

Mitchell shook his head in disgust. "Bishop showed you the bylaws?" he asked.

"Hell yeah," I replied. "Tried to tell us there was a right and wrong way of doing these things."

My friend nodded and stroked his chin goatee. "Yeah, they pulled that shit on me too. Fucking older brothers."

"They can shove the bylaws up their asses," Moody said, blue eyes flaring. "They don't give a shit about the bylaws—they're just trying to undermine us."

"Yup," Backstreet agreed, "this is more about political power than Goldman. Look at how many older brothers are here now. I bet they don't even want Goldman to be a brother, they just don't want us to wield any real power."

I stared at the large pack of older brothers and said, "If we have the revote now, I don't think we can get enough votes. Too many younger brothers are gonna be intimidated."

Klein was more optimistic. "We can still pull this off. Nobody likes this kid. We can get the votes."

Mitchell shook his head. "I don't know, man. After seeing him ball like a baby, there's gonna be a lot of sympathy votes."

"That's bullshit," I snarled. "That's not a way to build a brotherhood. I guarantee none of the kids who vote for him out of pity will ever hang out with him when he becomes a brother. He'll just be another Upsilon mistake they laugh at behind his back."

Mitchell turned to his auburn-haired roommate. "What do you think, Fish?"

Fish appeared thoughtful. "Some of the younger brothers are gonna be afraid to rock the boat. This is about a lot more than kicking out Goldman—it's about changing our entire philosophy."

I nodded. "It's about elitism which is another reason why a lot of our brothers don't support this—they aren't fucking elite."

Backstreet pulled a long drag from his cigarette and furiously exhaled smoke in the direction of the older brothers. A look of defiance burned strongly in his eyes.

"Fuck this shit," he said. "We should just walk out of here right now and not participate."

"No," replied Blake, whose own dark eyes were filled with recalcitrance. "We should demand this vote not even happen…*or else*."

Klein looked startled. "What are you talking about— Reorg?"

All eyes turned to Blake. Reorg was a forbidden word around Upsilon, but Blake smirked and irritably shrugged his shoulders.

"Whatever you want to call it," he answered. "Reorg would be better than letting them get away with this crap. I don't want to be in a fraternity that lets this kid in."

"Me neither," I agreed.

"Fuck that," Mitchell said. "We can't survive another Reorganization. We don't have the manpower or the finances. But Blake is right—we can't let these assholes pull this shit."

Although most of my friends shared this sentiment, we all feared that any effort to rally together an opposition to stand against the executive decision of the President of Upsilon would create a decisive rift with the fraternity that would not mend. Upsilon had already suffered through a National Reorganization caused by an unwanted pledge five years earlier. The result of that factious controversy gave birth to a new fraternity called Xi and was the primary reason why Upsilon was no longer the top fraternity on campus. It was unlikely that our fraternity could survive another Reorg.

A hush fell over the courtyard as Bishop and Lewis emerged from their apartment and solemnly walked across the concrete patio towards the basement. Brothers flicked out their cigarettes and filed into the basement to take a seat. The second blackball vote of Goldman was about to begin.

"Here we go," Mitchell said.

"Yeah," Blake grumbled. "Here we fucking go."

CHAPTER FIVE

ELITISM

"Everyone should want to be here."

Bishop and Lewis stood defiantly in front of the chapter. They knew they were causing a divisive controversy that threatened the future of our brotherhood, but they didn't care. Upholding their precious moral principles was more important than Upsilon's survival and prosperity.

"Please be seated," Bishop said to the chapter.

Most of the brothers were already sitting, but we quieted down and gave the President of Upsilon our full attention.

"The Executive Officers have given this a lot of thought and we've decided the importance of this vote demands it be conducted formally."

Jacob snorted. "If you guys don't like the outcome of the revote, are we gonna have a re-revote?"

Younger brothers snickered and older brothers frowned. My roommates and I boiled with anger. Bishop ignored the sarcastic remark and continued.

"The vote will be secret ballot. Two speakers will defend the pledge and two speakers will argue in favor of his blackballing. We'll give you a few minutes to decide who your speakers will be."

Very few were surprised that two older brothers assumed the duties of speaking in favor of Goldman's continuance as a pledge. Even fewer were surprised that Mitchell and I were chosen to speak against Goldman. According to convention, the defense team was given the first opportunity to speak.

A score of arguments were put forth by the older

brother to advance Goldman's case for brotherhood, but the three major points were: (1) It's not ethical to blackball Goldman this late in the semester—did you see the poor guy crying?; (2) He wants to be here and he's proven that by coming around a lot; (3) It's okay to let him become a brother because we've let pledges in before that didn't belong here.

My lip curled in disgust as I sat on a basement couch and listened to the older brother's pathetic arguments. These guys were fucking clueless about what it took to be a top level fraternity on campus. When it was my turn to speak, I angrily marched to the front of the Chapter and refuted the ideology of the older brothers.

"I've heard some of you here tonight argue that it's immoral to blackball a pledge this late in the semester."

Glancing around the room, I made eye contact with a few of the brothers who supported this argument. Their sympathy and pity for Goldman was something I understood and even felt, but that did not mean I endorsed the false conclusions they had drawn from these emotions.

"Gentlemen, we're not a charity, we're a brotherhood. We can't let tears stop us from doing what's necessary for the good of the fraternity. Our loyalty must be to ourselves first and foremost. Until Goldman becomes a brother, he's still an outsider and isn't owed the same degree of loyalty or respect you and I have for one another. We can pity the kid, but that doesn't mean he's earned the right to be treated as an equal."

The words that flowed from me were the accumulation of three semesters worth of frustration my friends and I had been forced to endure under the self-dooming guidance of the older brothers.

"Pledging is a trial period, not a guarantee of membership. One of the most important reasons we even have a pledging process is to test these kids out. Pledging isn't just about unity and bringing pledges together."

I paused to stare at a few of the brothers who believed

this to be the primary purpose of pledging.

"Sure, unity is important, but pledging is also about making these guys earn their brotherhood by proving to us they have something to offer. Has Goldman done this?"

I paused again for effect before bluntly answering my own question. "No, gentlemen, he has not. Goldman can't contribute anything to Upsilon except money and letting him wear our letters on campus will make all of us look bad."

My eyes searched the room, desperately looking for any kind of emotional reaction. Surely these words could be perceived as nothing but the truth. Surely they would convince more of my brothers to blackball Goldman. But most of the older brothers sat with arms crossed and sullen expressions on their faces and I realized my words had not even penetrated their thick skulls. Their decision had already been made and it had nothing to do with Goldman. To them, I was just an upstart younger brother whose ideas were challenging the dominance they wielded within the fraternity. To them, the ideas of the younger brothers would always be perceived as a threat, regardless of their content.

And yet, as I continued to look around the room, I did see faces of brothers who agreed with what I was saying. In the eyes of my closest friends, many of the younger brothers, and even a few of the older brothers—I saw the same sense of urgency and dissatisfaction that burned within me. They were frustrated with the status quo, they had the ambition to elevate the social reputation of our fraternity, and they were hopeful this goal was something that could still be achieved. Perhaps all was not lost. With more confidence, I continued to hammer away at Goldman's defense.

"Some of you think we shouldn't kick Goldman out because he wants to be here. Of course he wants to be here— the kid has nowhere else to go!"

A few brothers snickered at this remark. But it wasn't meant to be funny. It was the sad truth.

"Wanting to be here is important, but it's not enough to prove you deserve to be here. Everyone should want to be here. *That's* the kind of fraternity we should be trying to build."

Many brothers snapped their fingers in approval which caused the frowns of a few older brothers to grow longer. Good. These were the brothers beyond my ability to convince. It was the younger guys and the alpha males that I wanted on my side.

"Gentlemen, to become a brotherhood that everyone wants to join, we have to become a fraternity that not everyone can join. We have to pick the guys who can make this place better and improve our image on campus. Goldman can't do this."

The pure idiocy of the next argument I challenged never ceased to amaze me.

"I've heard some of you defend Goldman by saying it's okay to let him become a brother because we've made mistakes before. Yes, we've made mistakes before, but we should correct our mistakes instead of using them to justify making the same mistakes over and over again."

My final argument had to do with hazing and I believed it to be the most powerful argument I could make.

"Look, guys. The bottom line is this—we don't want Goldman to have the power to haze future pledge classes. Quality pledges would rather quit than be hazed by someone like him."

Thoughts of a toolbag older brother named Glenn entered my head. When I was a pledge, he had singled out Blake and me one night during a hazing session and we nearly quit the fraternity. Being hazed by a loser like him was bad enough, but being hazed by Goldman would be the absolute worst torture an alpha male could suffer.

"Gentlemen, ask yourselves this, if you were a pledge and Goldman was hazing you, would you stick out the semester or would you quit?"

I sat back down on the couch and waited for the next older brother to defend Goldman. It felt great to finally get everything off my chest by speaking aloud what most of the younger brothers thought to be wrong with Upsilon.

The second older brother speaking on Goldman's behalf recycled the same status quo arguments the older brothers always used to advance their clueless agenda. None of my counterpoints were addressed. It was as if he did not even listen to a word I said.

When it was Mitchell's turn to speak, he confidently strolled to the front of the room. Mitchell was a commanding presence in the fraternity whose handsome looks, magnetic sociability, and steadfast loyalty to his friends made him the embodiment of what a fraternity brother should be. His speech was more succinct than the one I gave, but brevity did not detract from the power of his message. After offering a few compelling arguments as to why Goldman should be denied brotherhood, he delivered the knockout blow.

With shrewd frankness, he openly declared, "I don't want a fraternity brother I would be embarrassed to introduce to my family or friends from back home."

No one laughed or made a sound. It felt like someone had just sucked the air out of the room. Mitchell's statement struck deep with those of us who were tired of being treated like second-class citizens on campus because of our association to a fraternity comprised of members who did not share our abilities to get ahead in the competitive social world of Tallahassee. The loyalty we had to our brotherhood was tremendous, but this did not change the fact that being the brother of a mediocre fraternity was an embarrassment.

When the speeches were over, a secret ballot vote was conducted to determine whether or not Goldman would be blackballed. Brothers were individually called forward to cast their vote by selecting a small polished stone and placing it into a ceramic black box. If a brother wanted the pledge to be blackballed, he put a black stone in the box. If he wanted Goldman to remain a pledge, a white stone was selected instead. After all of the brothers voted, Bishop carried the ceramic box towards the library where he and Lewis intended to tally the results behind closed doors. Many of the younger brothers were infuriated by this part of the secret ballot process.

Backstreet leapt up from his seat and yelled, "What the fuck? You're gonna sneak off and count the votes behind closed doors?"

"That's the way it's always done," Bishop answered with a startled expression.

"Fuck that!" Jacob screamed. "I don't care how it's always done. Count that shit out here for all of us to see."

Preston stared daggers at the two younger brothers as he scathingly asked, "You don't trust your president and vice-president?"

This was it. This was the moment of truth. Would the younger brothers risk the consequences of challenging an executive decision or would we trust our president and vice-president to do the right thing? More to the point, would we trust that they believed doing the right thing meant honestly counting the votes?

Backstreet sat back down. Silenced.

Jacob sat bock down. Silenced.

All of us sat back down. Silenced.

We squirmed in our seats like helpless children as Bishop and Lewis shut the double-doors of the library and started counting the votes. Minutes ticked away and tensions mounted. The large fraternity house basement that was usually filled with the sounds of laughter, cursing, and yelling was, for the first time that I could remember, completely silent. It was eerie. Everyone gathered in that room understood how consequential this vote would be to the future of our brotherhood. Two very different directions lay before us. Upsilon would either continue on the same path which would never rise above social mediocrity or we would follow a new course into uncharted waters.

Surely the vote would turn out in our favor. How could Mitchell and I not have swayed enough votes? How could anyone not see the truth in our words? But the more minutes that passed, the more I began to fear that we had failed to convince our brotherhood to implement the exclusionary policies of social elitism.

Bishop and Lewis emerged from the library and approached the Executive Table. It was impossible to determine from their blank faces which way the vote had gone, but I noticed they were not making eye contact with me or Mitchell. When Bishop finally spoke, his words were a sharp blade in my back.

"There were not enough votes to kick Goldman out of the fraternity. He stays."

Instant pandemonium. Older brothers cheered and younger brothers howled in rage.

"Fuck that shit!"

"This is bullshit!"

"That kid will never be my brother!"

"You fucking dumb-asses! This is why Upsilon can't get socials with the best sororities!"

"I'm fucking done with this place! Keep fucking fat chicks, you fucking losers!"

I sat there in momentary disbelief as the faction of brothers who voted to blackball Goldman cursed and stormed out of the basement. Two hours ago it had been the younger brothers who were gleeful and defiant in our victory, but now it was the older brothers who arrogantly shook each other's hands and laughed about their political triumph. That they could be so joyful in what I considered to be the lowest moment I had experienced as a member of Upsilon clearly demonstrated how different the goals of the younger brothers were from the older brothers. Without saying a word to anyone, my roommates and I left the fraternity house and drove home in bitter defeat.

Sitting in our living room five minutes later, Blake picked up the remote control and unpaused *Braveheart.* This time he did not recite any of the lines. We sat in silence, trying to come to grips with what just happened.

"You know," I finally said, "if a pledge interviewed me tomorrow and asked me what my best day in Upsilon was, I'd still answer the day we kicked Goldman out of the fraternity."

"You would?" Backstreet asked.

"Yup. But if they asked me what my worst day was, I'd say the exact same thing."

"Hell yeah," Blake replied. "Fuck the older brothers."

CHAPTER SIX

HELL WEEK

"Creed Speak!"

I entered the basement and stared at Timmy in disgust. The short pledge was standing in a pile of dark hair and his small hands were rubbing the back of his freshly shaved head.

"Why the fuck did you guys do that to him?" I asked. "We don't want him representing Upsilon on campus looking like Mr. Potato Head with glasses."

Rowdy and Jacob laughed, but they failed to detect the seriousness in my voice. Incredibly, the pledge didn't seem all that upset by the shaving of his head and he even cracked a silly smile.

Pebbles was also dragged into the basement by a pair of brothers. One of them snatched up the clippers.

"Don't shave his head," I urged. "We don't want these guys representing us, looking like shit."

"Fuck that," he said. "My head got shaved, so this motherfucker is getting his head shaved too."

I watched silently as they gave the round-faced pledge a mohawk before completely skinning his head. When they were finished, the kid's eyes started watering up.

"Are you crying like a bitch?" Rowdy asked.

Jacob pointed down at the new pile of dirty-blonde hair. "Sweep that shit up and throw it away!" he yelled.

The two other brothers laughed at Pebbles as he swept up the hair. I moved to the basement window and watched the pudgy kid carry the dust pan outside to the trashcans. Brothers in the courtyard heckled the humiliated young man as he used his free hand to wipe the tears out of his eyes.

"Cry, bitch boy!"

"Whaa! Whaa! Whaa!"

"What a fucking fag!"

"Pebbles, you're a fucking pussy!"

His tears revolted me. Being upset was one thing, but to actually cry was a pathetic display of weakness.

"What a bitch," Rowdy mumbled over my shoulder. "I can't believe he's fucking crying."

"Fucking pussy," I agreed.

"He shouldn't even be here," Rowdy said bitterly. "He should've been blackballed."

"Yup. Goldman and Timmy too."

My fraternity brother smiled wickedly. "It's not too late to get rid of them."

Two more pledges were in the basement library. They had just returned from class and were changing out of their sports coats and dress pants. When the young men emerged from the library wearing white t-shirts and red shorts, they were both laughing about something. This was a mistake—it was never a good idea to laugh during Hell Week.

Blake happened to be walking into the basement at that very moment and he was infuriated to hear this jovial sound coming from pledges who were supposed to be hating life right now.

"Creed Speak!" he snarled with flared nostrils.

The pledges straightened up tightly and immediately recited the Upsilon Creed. They would be required to do this many, many times throughout Hell Week, but on this particular occasion, one of the young men forgot to add the respectful "Sir" to the end of his recitation.

This discourtesy enraged my muscular roommate. He picked up a plastic chair and flung it at the two pledges who barely scurried out of the way in time. The faces of the young men paled with shock when they realized Blake had just tried to impale them with a blunt object.

"What the fuck is wrong with you!" Blake screamed at the pledges. "Get the fuck out of *my* basement!"

We all laughed as my roommate chased the terrified pledges out into the courtyard. Blake was truly a master of hazing. The heavy dose of wrath that existed deep inside him was one of the many reasons he and I got along so well. We both loved to hate.

I followed Blake out the door and observed ten of our pledges somberly gathered around a fire pit. The young men were duty-bound to keep the fire burning the entire Hell Week as a symbolic representation of the fire that burned within their hearts for Upsilon.

I laughed when I saw that Timmy was now duct-taped to one of the basketball posts. A cracked egg sat on his newly bald head and a few brothers were hazing him.

"Don't let that shit fall!" yelled Russo, a tough-looking Italian kid. "Keep that egg up there like your fucking life depends on it!"

The voice of Russo's brown-haired roommate Fangs was more comical. "Are you hungry, Timmy?" he asked. "Did your big brother remember to feed you today? Don't worry, if that egg falls, you're gonna eat if off the ground!"

"Fuck that!" Russo screamed in Timmy's face. "If it falls, he's eating that shit off Goldman's fat stomach!"

Fangs laughed and continued to taunt the pledge. "Do you want to eat it off your pledge bother's stomach? Huh? Do you?"

Timmy's eyes remained fixated on something behind the brothers. He knew what they were trying to do, arouse his emotions so that he involuntarily moved his head and caused the egg to fall. But he refused to be goaded.

The young man's stoic composure infuriated Russo. He reached out his hand and squeezed the cheeks of the pledge so that his face puckered up like a fish.

"You want to eat if off his stomach, don't you?" Russo

yelled. "Or maybe you want to eat it off his dick like a little faggot!"

The egg quivered precariously on the pledge's head and other brothers in the courtyard became excited.

"It's gonna fall!"

"It's gonna fall!"

"That shit's gonna drop!"

But it didn't fall. Not yet anyways.

I was pleased to see the courtyard was packed. One of the cool things about Hell Week was that brothers came out in great numbers to hang out and participate in the hazing of the pledges. Brothers you had not seen for months would even show up to partake in the Hell Week activities. Some of these long lost brothers came around because they truly missed the fraternity. Others just wanted to torment pledges.

Two inactive brothers named West and Shultz had shown up the previous night to participate in a hazing activity we called Space Invaders. In this brutal form of dodgeball, shirtless pledges lined up against the basement wall and flailed their arms up and down as they slowly moved towards a group of brothers standing fifteen yards away. These brothers took turns hurling balled up wet t-shirts at the pledges. Since West and Shultz were baseball players capable of throwing 90 mph fastballs, the wet t-shirts slung by the fearsome duo left a large welt on the unfortunate pledges beamed by their pitches. The loud smacking sound of a 90 mph wet t-shirt striking against bare skin was a truly awful noise to hear, but it was pretty damn funny to watch.

When I reached the far side of the courtyard, I sat down next to Moody on a long wooden bench. The athletically-built young man was wearing navy-blue Adidas gym shorts and a long-sleeved FSU football t-shirt.

He nodded at me. "What's up, man?"

"What's going on? You coming from the Leach?"

"Yeah, I just worked out with Klein."

"Where's he at now?"

"He went home."

I shook my head irritably. "That guy never hangs out around here. He's a fucking ghost bother."

"Yeah, he is," Moody grudgingly agreed, his blue eyes watching the pledges gathered near the fire pit. When my friend turned to face me, I noticed he seemed anxious.

"So, I got a problem," he said, "and I need some Bryce advice."

I was intrigued. The self-assured young man was not the type of guy who sought advice often.

"What's up? You got the HIV or something?"

Moody chuckled. "Nah, not yet. But you know I've been fucking Sara, right?"

"The blonde-haired waitress from Long Horn?"

"Yeah, the older one."

"Lucky bastard. Her body is *ridiculous*."

Moody grinned. "She's a freak too. Last night I was over at her place hooking up on the couch. We were about to fuck, but I had to grab a condom from my car. When I came back inside, she was waiting for me naked, bent over on all fours."

"You just walked in and there she was—ass up in the air?"

"Yeah," he replied, his grin growing wider.

"That's fucking awesome. So what's the problem?"

Moody hesitated, looked away, and then finally made eye contact again. "Her pussy smells," he said quietly.

I was shocked. You would never suspect a hot piece of ass like Sara to have this kind of problem. It was hard enough to imagine a sexy girl like that even taking a shit, let alone having a hygiene issue like an odorous smelling vagina.

My eyebrows arched with disbelief. "Bad?"

"Bad."

"*How* bad are we talking—sweaty armpit bad or Sushi

Koochie?"

"Fish. Raw fish."

I laughed my ass off.

"It's not funny, man," he said, shaking his head with a reluctant smile. "What the fuck do I do about it?"

"Do you go down on her?"

"I try not to...but yeah. I had to do it the first time to get laid and now she kind of expects it."

"Yeah, that's a rough situation. Maybe you should tell her to shave it all off. Those pubes can absorb smells."

"Her shit is baby clean."

"Damn. We're dealing with an internal issue then. You should just walk away now before you get any deeper involved." I sniffed my nose at him. "But it might already be too late. I can smell her funk on you right now."

"Fuck you," he sighed.

I stood up off the bench and shook my head in disbelief. "Wow," I said, "a hot girl like Sara has Stink Pussy...I need a cigarette."

Moody laughed as I walked away, but I don't think he thought it was very funny. How could he? A smelly vagina was an absolutely horrid thing to encounter. I can remember fingering this Asian girl one time and smelling her vagina on my fingers two days, four showers, and ten hand scrubbings later. No exaggeration. Stink Pussy is the worst. The first girl I ever went down on suffered this affliction, but since she was my first, I didn't know any better and repeatedly suffered through the experience much longer than I should have. That smell has haunted me for years and anytime I smell armpit, I think of her.

Mendez was sitting on the back steps and I sat down next to him.

"What's up, Bryce?" he said with a friendly nod.

"Sup. Do you have any smokes?"

The chubby-faced Latino pulled out a fresh pack of

Parliament Lights and handed me a cigarette.

I smiled. "Did you steal this pack from one of the pledges?"

Mendez nodded as he fired up a cigarette for himself and passed me the lighter.

"Thanks," I said.

"Those stupid fucks didn't have to bring any Big League Chew this year."

I lighted my own cigarette and shook my head in disappointment. Every semester the pledges were given a list of specific items they were required to bring with them to Hell Week. Tobacco products and Big League Chew were usually on the list and brothers always stole these items.

Mendez exhaled a cloud of smoke and said, "We should make the pledges bring two packs of cigarettes instead of chew. Nobody touches that shit."

"Not true," I replied. "Clayton made Goldman gobble up a big handful of chew yesterday."

"How'd he like it?"

I snorted. "His freckled face was turning green. All the rednecks were laughing their asses off."

Mendez chuckled. "Serves him right. I still can't believe that kid didn't get blackballed. Fuck the older brothers."

"Yeah...pretty much. So what's up with you and Vanessa? I heard you two are getting close these days."

"We've been hanging out a lot lately. She's a cool girl."

"Is it official?"

"Yeah," he said with macho reluctance, "she's my girlfriend."

I exhaled smoke and grinned. "Did you get Bounce's blessing?"

"Shit, I haven't talked to that guy since he left."

"Yeah, me neither. No one has. This time he really bounced the fuck out of here, so I guess you can't be held accountable for dating his ex."

"Bro, if a guy leaves town, doesn't call, doesn't write, and you never expect to see him again, he's not your real friend."

"No, he isn't," I replied sarcastically. "*Especially* if you're sticking your cock into his ex-girlfriend's pussy."

Mendez pulled a drag from his cigarette and shook his head. "Fuck you, Bryce. I like this girl. She's probably the first girl I've liked at FSU. Don't make me feel like a dick. Bounce is gone and he's not coming back."

Bounce was a pledge brother of ours who dated Vanessa for most of our freshman year. We nicknamed him Bounce because he was the first guy to disappear from every social event and he always left without telling anyone he was leaving. Like most of my pledge brothers, Bounce partied hard with drugs, but things got so bad his parents eventually yanked him out of school. Vanessa used to party with Bounce quite a bit, though I could never be sure of who was influencing who more.

"Does Vanessa still party like she used to?" I asked.

"Nah, we just chill out together. We smoke weed and spend a lot of time on the couch."

"That's cute. You guys cuddle and shit?"

Mendez glared at me. "You're full of jokes today, aren't you? Like *you're* one to talk."

"Haven't you heard? Your boy is single again."

"Now."

"Now," I repeated as thoughts of Alison swirled in and out of my head. I had actually spent the previous night with her, but we were still very much broken up and I had every intention to make sure it stayed that way.

I glanced to the far side of the courtyard to see if Timmy had dropped the egg yet. Some of the yolk was starting to ooze down his forehead.

"Hey, Timmy!" I yelled. "Maybe we should put you in a trashcan again!"

A few brothers laughed and the small face of the pledge tightened in reaction to my words.

"What'd you mean by that?" Mendez asked.

My lips twisted into a sly smile. "You weren't here for the Timmy trashcan episode?"

"Nah," he replied. "What happened?"

"I think the proper legal term is negligence. A few weeks ago we had a Call-In and we made the pledges play Hollywood Squares. The game—"

"Wait," he interrupted. "Hollywood Squares? Which one is that?"

"Tic-tac-toe with the trashcans."

Mendez's face lit up with humor. "Oh yeah! Hollywood Squares! So what happened?"

"When the game ended, we forgot Timmy was crouched inside one of the trashcans and whichever brother wheeled it back outside didn't realize the kid was in there because he doesn't weigh more than a buck twenty."

Mendez burst out laughing. "So he got left in there? For how long?"

"I don't know…at least twenty minutes." My gaze returned to the pledge duct-taped to the basketball post. "Hey, Timmy! How long were you in that trashcan?"

The young man said nothing and his eyes remained fixated straight ahead.

"Timmy!" I called out again in warning. "Do you really want to ignore me right now? How long were you in the fucking trashcan?"

The short pledge shifted nervously, and after a moment of hesitation, he shouted, "Sir, long enough to make me love Upsilon even more than I already did, Sir!"

"Fucking smartass," I mumbled with a soft chuckle.

The pledges gathered around the fire pit must have thought so too because they started laughing. Dumb fucks. It was never a good idea to laugh during Hell Week.

"Creed Speak!" I yelled furiously.

Timmy and the rest of his pledge class immediately recited our creed in unison. When they were finished, Mendez flicked his cigarette away and stood up.

"Screw this," he said. "It's time to put these kids through the washing machine."

My meathead fraternity brother disappeared into his lower-house apartment and returned moments later with a bottle of dish soap.

"Hey, Big Country! Raul!" Mendez screamed in the direction of the pledges standing near the fire pit. "Get one of the trashcans and bring it over here!"

The young men retrieved a trashcan and wheeled it over to where Mendez and I were now waiting in the middle of the courtyard. It was a large black trashcan with a white Greek letter Upsilon spray-painted on the side. I flipped opened the plastic lid and saw two trash bags, multiple beer cans, one rotten banana, and what looked like moldy french fries. It was perfect for what we were about to do.

"Hey, Goldman!" Mendez yelled. "Go get the fucking hose and bring it here!"

Goldman left his pledge brothers at the fire pit and scampered to the front building of the fraternity house to retrieve a grey hose. With both hands methodically working, he hurriedly unraveled the long hose from its hanging apparatus and then started dragging it across the courtyard.

"Turn the hose on first, dipshit!" I yelled.

The pledge dropped the hose and darted back to the faucet. You could tell he was trying extra hard to please all of the brothers during Hell Week.

I used the hose to fill up the trashcan while Mendez squeezed in half the bottle of dish soap. Bubbly trash water slowly began to rise. A couple minutes passed before I motioned Goldman towards the trashcan.

"Alright," I said. "Now climb in there."

A dumbstruck look formed on the pledge's freckled face, and for the first time since Hell Week had begun, he hesitated to do something a brother ordered him to do. *Good.* We had finally found his weakness—cold, bubbly, trash water.

"Don't fucking think about it!" I screamed at the pledge. "Just fucking do it!"

Goldman put his hands on the rim of the trashcan and again he hesitated. It dawned on me that the red-haired kid was trying to figure out how to climb into the large container without tipping over and falling on his skull.

Mendez snarled at Big Country and Raul. "What the fuck are you two doing? You're supposed to be showing us unity! Help him get in there!"

Raul stepped forward and held the trashcan steady. Big Country hunched over and interlocked his fingers together to make a step for Goldman. The freckle-faced young man stepped up onto the hands, clumsily swung his other leg over the rim of the trashcan, and slowly lowered his foot into the cold, soapy trash water.

I immediately lifted the hose and dripped it over Goldman's head and down the back of his t-shirt.

"Fuck!" the pledge gasped in surprise and obvious discomfort. Since it was a chilly afternoon in early December, the weather and water were cold enough to make his body shake with shivers.

"Shit's cold, isn't it?" Mendez asked.

The pledge nodded as he climbed completely inside the trashcan. When the bubbly trash water had risen nearly 2/3 of the way to the top, I dropped the hose on the ground and instructed Goldman to crouch down. The pledge obeyed and Mendez flipped the lid closed.

"This pledge is dirty!" I yelled. "Now his pledge brothers will clean him! Shake it up, boys!"

Our fraternity brothers cheered as I stepped back and motioned for Raul and Big Country to shake the trashcan.

The two pledges rocked it back and forth with very little physical exertion. It was a half-ass job.

Mendez snatched up the hose and sprayed the two pledges in punishment. They both flinched at the chilling impact of the cold water and gave Mendez a furious stare.

"Don't fucking bullshit us," Mendez warned the pledges as he threateningly waved the hose. "Shake it fucking hard or I'll make you get in there with him!"

This time Raul and Big Country rocked the trashcan with much more effort. Brothers cheered in delight as the two biggest guys in the pledge class shook the hell out of the trashcan for a good thirty seconds.

Mendez and I laughed wickedly when we heard the thumping sound of Goldman flopping around in there with the trash water. It really did sound like a washing machine.

"Alright," I said. "That's good. Now open it up."

The two pledges flipped over the plastic lid and a soapy-faced Goldman popped up like a jack-in-the-box.

"My eyes!" he screamed. "They're burning! They're burning!"

"I'm melting! I'm melting!" Moody mocked Goldman in the facetious tone of the Witch of Oz.

Brothers laughed hysterically and a chuckling Mendez put his thumb over the end of the hose to spray a powerful stream directly into Goldman's face. The pledge flinched in pain, but he was successfully able to cleanse his eyes of soap.

"Let this be a lesson to you, dumb-asses," Mendez declared to the pledges fretfully watching the spectacle from the fire pit. "Don't open your eyes in the washing machine!"

Brothers laughed and demanded another Goldman cleaning. After forcing the kid to endure his second round of the washing machine, we put a few more of the pledges through the same treatment until Moody got bored and decided to bum rush the trashcan

"Fuck pledges!" he screamed and kicked the plastic

container over with a pledge inside.

The large trashcan came crashing to the ground and the pledge tumbled out with a stream of soapy trash water. Moody, me, and the rest of our brothers laughed our asses off and all of the pledges were ordered to clean up the mess while Mendez sprayed them down with the hose. When the shivering pledge class had cleaned up the sludge, we told them to go warm up by the fire.

CHAPTER SEVEN

MONSTER

"Let me see it!"

Rap music thumped from Backstreet's black truck as we pulled into the gravel parking lot of the Upsilon House. Mitchell was already there waiting for us, standing like a sentry in front of his red Ford Ranger.

"Sup, kid?" Blake called out as he opened his door.

Mitchell responded with a tough guy head nod.

"I'm fucking amped up," Backstreet said as he climbed out of the truck. "Tonight is gonna be brutal."

Blake and Mitchell shook hands and laughed at the words of their fraternity brother.

"Hell yeah, yo," Blake said. "I'm gonna haze the shit out of these fucking kids."

Sitting in the flatbed of the truck, I smoked the last of a cigarette before flicking it away. The fun and games of Hell Week were over. It was time to get down to business. It was time to get rid of Goldman, Pebbles, and Timmy.

I hopped out of the truck with a case of beer in hand. It was going to be an intense night of hazing and we were all dressed accordingly. I wore camouflage pants, combat boots, and a black wife beater. Blake and Backstreet were similarly dressed in camouflaged pants and black wife beaters. Mitchell wore camouflage pants, but instead of a beater, he sported a tight black t-shirt stretched across his thin muscular frame.

I tossed beers to my partners in crime and cracked one open for myself. We raced to chug them down and smiled at each other wickedly.

"You ready to do this shit?" I asked.

"Fuck yeah," Blake replied. "These kids are dead."

Mitchell nodded. "It's now or never, boys. Now or never."

Backstreet flicked his tongue ring and said, "We're gonna break these fuckers tonight. Goldman, Timmy, and Pebbles are fucking history."

Blake had a fat dip of Skoal in his lip. He spit tobacco to the gravel parking lot and shook his head.

"I swear to fucking god," he said, "if those three pledges become brothers, I'm gonna burn this house down."

"They'll quit," Mitchell answered. "If we haze the shit out of them, they'll quit tonight."

Blake shook his head and spit tobacco. "I guarantee Goldman won't be the first to quit."

"Are you serious?" Mitchell asked in surprise. "He's the weakest one."

"That's why it won't be him. He needs this place more than the others do. Think about it. Any guy who didn't quit after all that blackball drama ain't gonna fucking quit because we haze him."

Mitchell nodded grudgingly. "Yeah…you're probably right. So we haze him just for fun and we haze the others until they break."

Blake passed out another round of beers and we chugged them. When some of the alcohol dripped down the side of my face, I used the back of my hand to wipe it dry.

"Fuck Goldman," I said. "We'll use him to mind-fuck the pledges—some divide and conquer kind of shit."

"I like it," Backstreet replied as he crumpled up his beer can and tossed it across the parking lot. "We'll punish all of them for *his* weakness. You know that pussy bitch is gonna drag ass in there."

"Without a doubt," Mitchell agreed. "Without a fucking doubt."

"Gentlemen," I said solemnly, "there can be no holding back tonight. What we're about to do, we do for the good of our fraternity. This is what it means to be a brotherhood."

My friends grunted in agreement and we spent the next thirty minutes devising hazing strategies as we killed the case of beer. When the alcohol was gone, we proceeded to the courtyard of the fraternity house.

"We're gonna need more beer," I said to my boys as we walked. "Someone should make another run."

"Don't worry about it," Backstreet replied as he shoved a cigarette in his mouth. "I'll take care of it later."

"Thanks, yo," Blake said as he eyed his brother with respect. My two competitive roommates had been getting along extremely well ever since the Goldman blackball incident. Their newfound solidarity reminded me of the ancient warrior code: *The enemy of my enemy is my friend.*

We entered the dark fraternity house courtyard which was illuminated by the ceremonial fire pit. Thirty pledges stood around the flames, all of them uniformly dressed in jeans, white t-shirts, and sneakers. Brothers were scattered around the house, smoking cigarettes and drinking beers as they watched the pledges from the shadows.

"Pledges!" I yelled. "Into the basement! NOW!"

The pledges scurried into the basement and my brothers followed. I intended to put the pledges through a demanding session of calisthenics. To create an unwelcoming ambience for the pledges, we turned off all the lights, ran a strobe light, and used Mag-Lite flashlights to blind the pledges when we screamed in their faces.

"Alright, bitches!" I yelled. "Grab a fucking weight and sit on the fucking wall!"

The pledges picked up plated weights, put their backs to the wall, and sat down on air.

"Up!" I screamed.

Arms came up and the pledges held the weights out in front of their chests.

"Creed Speak!"

And so it began. Pledges recited the Upsilon Creed and the Greek alphabet over and over again as shoulders and legs were slowly worn down. When they were beginning to show signs of exhaustion, I had them lie down on their stomachs to do pushups. This hazing exercise was particularly unpleasant because the floor stunk of mung—the buckets of ketchup, vinegar, rotten eggs, and sour milk we dumped on the pledges the first night of Hell Week. Since many of the pledges had vomited from this torturous experience, the stench that permeated from the floor was particularly vile.

"Up!" I yelled. "Down!"

"One!" screamed the pledges in unison.

"Up!" I yelled. "Down!"

"Two!"

"Up! Down!"

"Three!"

This continued on until they hit twenty and I spotted Goldman dipping his knees to do girly pushups. The freckle-faced pledge always struggled with physical hazing which led me to believe he had never seen the inside of a gym before—one of the many reasons I did not want him in my fraternity.

"Goldman is cheating on you!" I screamed at the pledges. "He's doing little girl pushups while you suffer through the real thing! If you can't work together as a unit, then you'll be punished as a unit!"

Goldman raised his knees off the floor and all of the pledges listened anxiously for the command to lower their bodies to the down position. But that command did not come. Seconds passed and then seconds turned into minutes.

"Keep holding up!" I yelled.

Exhausted pledges suffering from sleep and food deprivation strained to hold their bodyweight off the ground. It was not long before butts shot up in the air as pledges tried to shift some of their body weight from their shoulders and pecs to their legs.

"Get your fucking asses down!" Backstreet screamed as he put his foot on the ass of a pledge and shoved it. "Are you a bunch of faggots? Get your asses down now!"

Butts lowered and the faces of pledges showed increased strain as their shoulders and chests were once again forced to endure a heavier burden of their bodyweight. Thirty more seconds passed before I finally relented.

"Down!" I yelled.

The young men slumped to the floor in relief, but my mercy would be short-lived.

"Now, on your backs! Legs six inches off the ground!"

Pledges groaned as they rolled onto their backs and elevated their straightened legs into the air. A few pledges were slow to obey.

"Anderson and Julian!" Mitchell screamed. "Get your fucking legs up right now!"

Blake was stomping back and forth behind the pledges, snarling and cursing down at the ones he did not like.

"Fuck you, Timmy!" he yelled. "Quit groaning, you fucking bitch! Goldman, keep your legs still or I'll fucking break em!"

Blake loved to haze. Like me, he had a lot of anger buried deep inside him. I knew the source of my rage, but Blake's demons were his own and I never asked him about them. Maybe his anger had something to do with his abandonment by his natural parents. Or maybe he was just a natural born killer.

"Down!" I yelled and legs fell to the ground.

"Up!"

Legs came back up and I smiled. Six inch leg lifts were a favorite hazing activity of mine. To increase the intensity of this abdominal exercise, I armed myself with a pool stick and swung it rapidly under the legs of the pledges. Any pledge who made the mistake of lowering his legs early would get whacked painfully with the stick. No one was surprised when the stick eventually struck Goldman in the calf.

"Ahhh!" Goldman yelped in pain.

"You fucking pussy!" Blake screamed as he dropped down to all fours and barked in the kid's face. "Why the fuck would I want a pussy like you to be my brother? I fucking hate you! Get your legs up! Get em up! Get em up!"

The pledge struggled to hold his feet six inches off the ground and I continued to swing the pool stick underneath his legs, daring him to lower them again. Goldman may have been the weak link, but Blake was right, there was no way this kid was quitting. Timmy and Pebbles were our prey tonight.

"Down!" I finally shouted and the legs of the pledges dropped to the ground with thuds. "Alright, back on the wall with your weights!"

Pledges cursed and groaned as they climbed to their feet and returned to the basement wall. They picked up the plated weights, and then with their backs against the wall, sat down on air, holding themselves up with their leg muscles.

"Up!" I yelled.

The pledges straight arm lifted the ten pounds weights to chest level.

"Down!"

Weights lowered and the young men shouted, "One!"

"Up!" I yelled. "Down!"

"Two!"

"Up! Down!"

"Three!"

Over and over again, I forced the pledges to lift and lower the weights as their legs slowly endured the increasing weariness of holding up their bodyweight. When I was certain their shoulders were exhausted, I let them lower the weights to their laps. Then, like a drill sergeant, I paced in front of the long line of pledges to inspect their condition.

They looked extremely fatigued and a few faces showed signs of contempt. Good. I wanted them to hate me because hatred would give them strength to endure or it would seduce them to quit.

"You look tired, pledges," I said with a calm but mocking tone. "You look like you don't want to be here. Who wants to go home?"

None of the pledges replied.

"Alright," I asked, "then who wants to keep sitting on the wall? Because those are the only two choices in front of you. Quit now or sit on the wall. Which will it be?"

Silence again.

Brothers were growing restless. They wanted to haze and they wanted to haze right now. Backstreet suddenly rushed forward into Pebbles' face.

"Alphabet Speak you piece of shit pledge!" he yelled.

The pledges all shouted, "Alpha-beta-gamma-delta-epsilon-zeta-eta-theta-iota-kappa-lambda-mu-nu-xi-omicron-pi-rho-sigma-tau-upsilon-phi-chi-psi-omega-Sir!"

"Again!" I screamed. "Alphabet Speak!"

As they recited the Greek alphabet, I continued to walk up and down the long line of pledges. There was definitely defiance in their eyes, but there was also exhaustion, and in some faces, I thought I even detected the distant fear of failure. *Good.* It was time to escalate things.

"Up!" I yelled. "Now hold it!"

The young men lifted the plated weights up and away from their bodies. Since their shoulders were already tired, it was not long before I began to see signs of struggle.

"Creed Speak!" I yelled.

The pledges chanted the Upsilon Creed and brothers watched them feverishly, like coiled up rattlesnakes ready to strike. When the druidic recitation was over, Goldman lowered the ten pound weight to his waist. Mitchell reacted instantly by pouring beer on the pledge's head and cursing in his face.

"You're fucking worthless, Goldman!" he yelled. "Get

your fucking weight up!"

Pebbles too had made the mistake of lowering his weight and Backstreet slammed his fist against the wall, inches from the pledge's head.

"Get that fucking weight up!" he screamed. "Get it up, you goddamn pussy!"

I smiled. It was time to divide and conquer.

"Gentlemen," I said, "your pledge brothers Goldman and Pebbles lowered their weights. This means all of you have to do thirty more seconds!"

Several pledges cussed furiously at their weaker pledge brothers who flinched at the rebuke. Thirty more seconds passed and weights began to wobble.

"Down!" I yelled.

The arms of the pledges came down quickly, but there was no relief in their young faces because leg muscles were beginning to struggle as the physical exertion of performing wall-sits began to take its toll. And I was nowhere near ready to call it quits. Timmy or Pebbles were going to break tonight and they were going to break right now.

"Up!" I screamed.

The weights lifted in unison and I marched down the line of pledges.

"Who wants to go home?" I asked. "Who wants to go home right fucking now and take a hot shower?"

No one answered.

Blake stepped forward and asked, "Who wants to sleep in a real bed tonight instead of sleeping on the floor of a fucking bathroom?"

The pledges strained to hold the weights in the air, but none of the young men faltered.

Mitchell stepped forward and yelled, "I know one of you little bitches wants to quit! Why don't you just go home?"

"We are home!" Big Country shouted.

"Down!" I yelled.

"That's what we're looking for!" Mitchell exclaimed. "That's the dedication we want from you!"

He rewarded Big Country by tilting his beer and pouring it into the pledge's mouth instead of on his head.

Mitchell was right. The mentality we wanted pledges to ascertain during Hell Week was that the fraternity house was their home and we were their family. Under normal circumstances, I would have ended the hazing session right then and there because this important lesson had obviously been learned, but I continued to haze the pledges because I was convinced that Timmy or Pebbles would break.

"Up!" I yelled. "Creed Speak!"

The ten pound plated weights came up and I marched back and forth in front of the pledges as they chanted the Upsilon Creed. My eyes hawkishly watched for someone to lower their weight prematurely, but to my surprise, none of the young men faltered. It was time to mind-fuck them.

This time I spoke loudly, but calmly, without aggression or hostility.

"I know that some of you are thinking about quitting, but you think quitting now would be a waste. You're calculating in your heads how far you've come and how you only have to survive a little bit longer until you finally become an Upsilon brother."

I laughed loudly. It was a deep and evil laugh and all the brothers in the basement started laughing too.

"Gentlemen," I continued, "let me educate you how wrong you are. What day is it today, Mitchell?"

"Day three," he answered.

"And how many days are in a *week*?"

"Seven," he sneered at the pledges.

I whirled on the pledges and unleashed the beast once more. "Seven fucking days!" I screamed. "Seven fucking days! That means you have four more days of dealing with this shit! Four more days of calisthenics! Four more days of bitch work!

Four more days of food and sleep deprivation! Do you think you can fucking handle it?"

There were actually only two more days left, but Hell Week was always far more difficult for pledges to mentally endure if they believed it lasted a full seven days.

My foreboding words seemed to have the desired effect I was looking for. Timmy's skinny little arms began to shake like crazy and his eyes filled with panic. Combat boots clunked on the floor as I charged for the wavering pledge.

"Don't you fucking drop it!" I yelled. "Don't you fucking do it!"

Timmy's lips tightened as he mentally struggled against the law of gravity.

"Don't be a fucking pussy!" I screamed in his face. "Let me see the monster within you! Let me see the fucking monster!"

Timmy's jaw clenched together and his cheek muscles bulged. There was unadulterated hatred in his eyes. Hatred of me, hated of being hazed, hatred of that ten pound weight in front of him, but most of all, hatred of the weakness inside him that was going to let the weight fall. But the wobbling weight did not lower and I continued to yell in his face.

"That's it, Timmy! Let me see it! Show me the fucking monster!"

Rage burned in his eyes and the eighteen-year-old pledge became so fired up he started screaming like a wild animal. The eerie shriek sounded like the cry of a sacrificial lamb being stabbed with a knife. With his mouth wide open letting out this horrible sound, he repeatedly slammed his shave head against the wall, banging the plaster so hard he put a large dent in it.

"Down!" I yelled. "Put the weights on the ground and go back outside by the fire!"

The pledges obeyed my orders and swiftly fled out the basement door. Someone flicked on the lights and brothers investigated the fresh dent in the wall.

"Holy shit, Bryce," Mitchell said. "You just turned Timmy into a man!"

"Show me the monster!" Backstreet growled like a pro wrestler and flexed his muscles. "Show me the fucking monster!"

My brothers laughed, but I moved to the doorway and quietly watched Timmy standing near the fire pit. I was duly impressed. Maybe there was a warrior lurking somewhere inside this puny specimen of a man. Maybe I had underestimated Timmy and what he could contribute to my fraternity. The short pledge had clearly reached his breaking point—but he did not break. I might have given him a little push, but it was he who dug deep inside himself and found strength that he never knew he had.

I was proud of Timmy. He had proven to me he was willing to fight for my fraternity and this was all I really wanted from my brothers. Hanging out with good-looking, popular guys might get you laid by the hottest girls on campus, but no fidelity among men is greater than the tribal loyalty of men willing to fight for one another. When word spread about Timmy's passionate display of determination, he was given the respect he had rightfully earned and was never picked on again.

Pebbles would receive no such solace. With Goldman and Timmy no longer on our hit list, the chubby pledge was forced to endure the blunt of our hazing and the apex of this cruelty was reached later that night—The Night of the Bull.

CHAPTER EIGHT

THE CRUELTY OF MEN

"GET THE FUCK OUT OF MY HOUSE!!!"

"Come on, Pebbles!"

"Hurry up, you chubby fuck!"

"You get to ride with us tonight!"

"Don't worry. We're gonna treat you *real* good!"

"Are you ready to use that condom in your pocket?"

"Maybe I should use it on you!"

"Get in the car!"

"Get your ass in there!"

"Put this blindfold on!"

"Tight!"

"Tighter, you fucking bitch!"

"This is it, Pebbles! This is the night it happens!"

"Are you ready to prove to us you want to be here?"

"Are you ready for the Night of the Bull?"

We all grunted and mooed like cows.

"Creed Speak, you piece of shit!"

The Night of the Bull was always the worst night of hazing. Blindfolded pledges were driven out to the woods and force-marched through bushes, shrubbery, and a small creek with water up to their waists. Dirt was kicked on them and branches were used to scratch and strike them. If a pledge let go of the pledge's shoulders in front of him, he was cursed at and physically abused by drunk brothers. The forced march was periodically halted so that blindfolds could be removed and a brief ceremony could take place in which the pledges were taught the secrets of Upsilon. During these rituals, the Executive Officers wore red and white priestly-looking robes as they solemnly read from the sacred texts of the fraternity.

After the final ceremony, the blindfolded pledges were herded together near a large bonfire. It was time to face the bull.

"Hell yeah," Blake whispered to me from where we stood watching. "I love this part."

"They're gonna piss themselves," I said.

"Pebbles will probably fucking cry again."

"Probably."

"Where the hell is Slackjaw?"

"Right there. He's about to talk to them."

The Pledge Marshall stepped forward to face down his pledges. By all accounts, Slackjaw was not an imposing figure. He stood at about 5ft 9, had short brown hair, a pronounced chin, and a squirmy way of talking. His build was average and his personality tame. The fact that he was not intimidating reduced the authority of his position, but that didn't really matter tonight. A mouse could have played his role and would still have been menacing.

"Alright, pledges!" he yelled. "I want you to pull out the condoms you have in your front pockets!"

His voice was followed by the terrifying noise of a large bull mooing in agitation. Hooves pounded on metal and the animal grunted in frustration.

"Shut that big fucker up!" screamed a brother.

"Settle him down!" yelled another. "Settle him the fuck down!"

"Are you ready?" the Pledge Marshall hollered at the pledges. "Are you ready to prove you'll do anything to join Upsilon? Are you read to fuck a bull?"

The bull mooed louder in agitation and his hooves clanged on the metal surface again. Some of the blindfolded pledges flinched in fear.

"Drop your pants!" yelled the Pledge Marshall. "Drop your pants and start jerking your little dicks right now to get them hard!"

Blake and I continued to stomp on the flatbed of

Mitchell's truck. My combat boots were particularly effective at simulating the sound of hooves clanging on metal. Mitchell sat in the front seat of the truck and was controlling the stereo. Loud grunting and mooing sounds continued to drone from the audio speakers. It was all an act and we were the starring actors.

"Look at Curtis jacking his little dick!" Blake said to me with a giggle.

"Look at Zach!" I exclaimed. "Asians really do have tiny fucking cocks!"

About half the pledge class had dropped their pants and were manually stimulating themselves or trying to put condoms on their limp dicks. Those that did not stood like statues with hands defiantly held behind their backs.

"You fucking bitches!" a brother suddenly screamed.

"You fucked up!" yelled another. "You fucked up bad!"

"You're the worst fucking pledge class I've ever seen!"

Cursing brothers fell upon the blindfolded pledges like a pack of wolves. Many of the young men tried to pull their pants up and were prevented from doing so by brothers who dragged them off into the night.

"Fuck you, pledge!" brothers were yelling. "Fuck you!"

"You fucking suck! You fucking suck!"

"You screwed up, man! You guys are fucking morons!"

Some of the pledges were yelled at for failing to drop their pants.

"What the hell, Curtis? Don't you want to be a brother of Upsilon?"

"I thought you had heart, bitch! I thought you had fucking heart!"

"You're supposed to be willing to do anything!"

Others were chastised for dropping their pants.

"You sick fuck! Do you think we want pledges that have sex with farm animals?"

"You fucking idiot! You'd really fuck a bull in the ass?"

Others still were yelled at for the failure of the pledge class to act like a cohesive unit.

"Unity, bitch! Unity! You're supposed to act like the member of a brotherhood. We don't want loners!"

Yelled at, cursed at, and berated, the pledges were all dragged back to the cars. Pebbles was forced to ride in Moody's SUV so that my roommates and I could verbally abuse him. Sadistic heavy metal music blasted from the speakers as we all hazed the blindfolded pledge with venomous words of cruelty.

"What the fuck is wrong with you, Pebbles? Don't you get it yet?"

"You don't belong here!"

"You don't deserve to be in our fraternity!"

"Do you fucking understand me? You're not wanted!"

"YOU'RE NOT WANTED!"

"Creed Speak!"

We were drunk, we were emotional, and we believed the ends justified the means. The pledge did not belong in the fraternity we were trying to build because his presence among us would inhibit our brotherhood from achieving social status ascension. If we were ever going to stop Pebbles from becoming an Upsilon brother, then it was now or never. *Now or never.*

"We don't want you here!"

"You don't belong! You don't fucking belong!"

"Why the fuck would we want *you* wearing *our* letters!"

Overwhelmed with raw emotion, Blake suddenly threatened, "I fucking hate you, Pebbles! I fucking hate you! I'll kill your family!"

Blake was an adopted child, so this was probably the cruelest thing he could think of saying to someone. It was enough. The pudgy-faced pledge ripped off his blindfold and started squealing like a stuck pig.

"Stop! Stop! Stop!" he wailed with tears in his eyes.

"Let me out of the car! Let me out! Stop the fucking car! Now! Now! Now!"

Moody pulled the white SUV to the side of the road and Blake climbed out of the vehicle. Pebbles scrambled out behind him and staggered away, his upper-body violently convulsing with the sobbing spasms of a broken man.

We did it! We fucking did it!

Now all we had to do was figure out how to get him back into the car. It took some coddling, but Pebbles eventually climbed back in the SUV. The vehicle pulled back onto the road and we resumed our journey home. No one said a word until Backstreet turned around to face the tormented pledge.

"Are you quitting?" he asked.

Pebbles stared out the window, refusing to make eye contact with any of the assholes in the car who had treated him with such degrading contempt. But he nodded his head and replied with a sullen whisper of a voice.

"Yes," he said, "I'm quitting."

We rode the rest of the way home in silence. There was no need to haze the pledge anymore. Our mission was a success.

The ambiance of the Upsilon House was extremely antagonistic to pledges when we arrived. A few of the young men were lying in the gravel parking lot where brothers cursed down at them and repeatedly kicked rocks on them. Others had been sent under the courtyard deck to play Cockroach. This meant they were forced to slither around the crawlspace and stick little twigs up through the cracks of the wooden deck floor as they called out in high-pitched voices, "Don't step on me! I'm a little cockroach!" Brothers would stomp wherever the twigs appeared. Thirty yards away, pledges were defending the fire pit from assault by brothers trying to put it out with water. Other brothers furiously warned the pledges that if the fire burned out, they would be blackballed from the fraternity. In addition to these hazing activities, a handful of pledges were being subjected to grueling calisthenics in the basement.

Cruelty can spread like fire among men. Within seconds, the contagious atmosphere of hazing sucked in Blake and Backstreet. As Moody and I led Pebbles through the courtyard, my roommates followed closely on his heels.

"You're fucking worthless!" Blake yelled.

"That's right!" Backstreet screamed. "Quit, bitch!"

"We don't want you!"

"Get the fuck out of my fraternity!"

"You're a fucking loser, Pebbles! You're a fucking piece of shit loser!"

Moody mumbled to me in a disapproving tone. "This shit is getting out of hand. I don't want anything more to do with this."

My friend did not follow me into the basement, and once inside, I also stood back from the hazing. I felt guilty and ashamed of what we were doing. Things were spinning out of control and I was to blame more than anyone else because I had been the main architect of the exclusionary policies that the younger brothers were trying to enforce. For the first time, I began to question what we were doing and what we were trying to accomplish. More importantly, I began to question what moral cost I was willing to pay in order to achieve our goal of making Upsilon the best fraternity of campus.

Pebbles entered the basement and headed towards the library. His face looked ghostly pale, as if he was returning from a battlefield rather than the ceremonial hazing session of a college fraternity. I felt pity for the young man and wanted to end his suffering, but with the wolf pack of Blake and Backstreet right on his tail, no mercy was in sight.

My roommates were in an uncontrollable rage. When the pledge entered the library to gather his belongings,

Backstreet and Blake ripped away his two bags and hurled them out into the main chamber. The bags hit the wall and fell to the ground with thuds.

"GET THE FUCK OUT OF HERE!!!" Backstreet screamed in the pledge's face.

Blake chased after one of the bags and kicked it towards the door. With extreme hatred in his black eyes, he whirled around to face the stunned pledge and pointed towards the door.

"GET THE FUCK OUT OF MY HOUSE!!!" he screamed.

Pebbles furiously swept up his bags and marched out the door, fully prepared to leave the fraternity and its asshole brothers behind him forever. Midway through the courtyard, the pledge suddenly came to a halt.

I don't know why he stopped. Maybe Pebbles realized he had come way too far to quit or perhaps he dug deep within himself and found a source of pride that refused to let assholes like us bully him out of the fraternity.

When my roommates saw Pebbles standing still, they nearly charged out the basement door, but Bishop had already approached the pledge.

"Pebbles," he asked, "are you okay?"

The teary-eyed young man stared uneasily at the brother and did not reply.

"Pebbles, I'm not gonna haze you. That's not who I am. I just want to know if you're okay."

My roommates and I watched them together, unable to hear their words, but it was clear even from a distance that the President of Upsilon was nurturing the young pledge with kind words of encouragement.

The guilt I was feeling vanished and my anger instantly returned. I remembered that this battle of wills being waged with Pebbles was part of a much larger war of ideology being fought against the older brothers. And in every war, innocents must always suffer.

Lewis joined the conversation and took Pebbles somewhere inside the house to shelter him from the hazing. Meanwhile, Bishop entered the basement to talk to us.

"Listen up, guys," he said. "I don't want Pebbles to be hazed anymore tonight. I'm calling an end to all of this. Tonight's activities are over."

"Fuck that and fuck you!" Blake cursed.

He kicked open the basement door and stormed out into the courtyard. Backstreet and I followed our roommate, equally incensed by the intervention of the two brothers. Time and time again, meddling older brothers obstructed the progress we were working so hard to achieve.

The president hurriedly chased after us and spoke with a degree of politeness that only a natural pacifist could muster in this type of heated situation.

"Blake," he asked, "can I please talk to you guys? Can you come down to my apartment?"

"Yo, I ain't got shit to say to you," Blake snarled.

"There's *nothing* to talk about," Backstreet agreed.

Our president turned to me with pleading brown eyes and said, "Bryce? Please. This is important."

I looked at my roommates and sighed. "Alright. Fine. Let's get this over with."

With sullen expressions on our faces, we followed Bishop into his fraternity house apartment and sat down on the living room couches. The muscular shoulders of my roommates were rapidly moving up and down as they huffed and puffed from the visceral display of cruelty I had just witnessed. Bishop also noticed their heavy breathing.

After a few seconds of hesitation, he asked, "Not that this matters…and I'm not saying your behavior tonight was affected by it…but are the three of you on steroids?"

"Fuck you," Blake replied with a sneer.

Backstreet snorted and shook his head. "You *would*

think that, wouldn't you?"

Blake and Backstreet resented Bishop for asking this question, but in his defense, the three of us clad in camouflage pants and black wife beaters were not very shy about flexing our muscles which along with our aggressive hostility did fit the juicer stereotype. But none of us were on steroids at this point in time and I was the only one in that room who had even touched juice before.

I made eye contact with Bishop and said, "No, we're not on steroids and I'm insulted that you'd even ask me that."

"Well, you're all big guys…and tonight…" Bishop paused, searching for the courteous way to say that our actions resembled the roid rage mentality.

I spared him the trouble. "Look, man. You know we go to the gym every day, we supplement, and we eat right."

"Yeah, but you guys are all so muscular. And Bryce— *you* look like you've put on twenty pounds since the beginning of the semester."

"I probably have put on twenty pounds, but I was just putting on size that I lost from breaking my hand this summer. Remember? I broke my hand on some kid's skull."

I thought it might be helpful to remind Bishop that I was not disinclined to punching people in the face with whom I was quarreling, but the topic of violence reminded Bishop of something else that increased his suspicions.

"What about the other night?" he asked. "When you and Blake were destroying the basement, what was that all about?"

I exchanged a quick look with Blake and we shared an evil laugh. "Nah, man," I said, "that was nothing…we were just really wasted that night."

Shifting uncomfortably in his seat, Bishop decided to try a more direct approach by asking, "Did one of you guys threaten to kill Pebbles' family tonight?"

"Hell no," I immediately lied.

"That's total bullshit," Backstreet declared.

Blake did not respond. Leaning forward with his elbows resting on his knees, he sat quietly on the couch and attempted to exhibit the composure of an innocent man. He might as well have been twiddling his thumbs and whistling.

Bishop did not appear convinced, but at this point I didn't give a shit because the alcohol I consumed earlier in the night was wearing off and my patience was running thin.

"Look, Bishop," I said, "I know you're a man of your principles and that you don't personally agree with hazing or exclusionary policies. But what happened tonight was as much your fault as it was ours. We tried to get these guys out by blackballing them and then you went over our heads on a technicality to save Goldman."

"Yeah," Blake said, "You should've known this was gonna fucking happen."

"But it's not right," Bishop replied with the conviction of someone who believed he held the moral high ground. "It's not right to treat people this way."

"Not right for whom?" Backstreet asked. "It might not be right for them, but what we did tonight was for the good of the fraternity."

"But we shouldn't have to compromise our principles."

"What principles?" I challenged. "The day I swore an oath of allegiance to this fraternity is the day I decided to place a higher value on my brothers than anyone outside our brotherhood. *That's* the principle I'm trying to uphold and stand by."

We continued to argue our positions back and forth, but for both sides it was a hopeless effort. At the end of the day, when it boils down to it, there is no common ground between liberal idealists like Bishop who believe there exists some great universal humanity among men that necessitates all people be valued equally, and practical realists like us who believe that in order to survive and prosper in a competitive world, you must be willing to put the interest of your family, brotherhood, and nation before the interests of outsiders.

Unable to resolve our opposing worldviews, we agreed to disagree and my roommates and I left the apartment.

Outside in the courtyard, it looked like things had calmed down. Most of the pledges were standing around the fire pit and several groups of brothers were scattered around the house, smoking cigarettes and quietly laughing.

"Fucking asshole." Blake mumbled as we strolled through the courtyard. "I hate that guy."

I shrugged dismissively. "He's just driven by a different concept of morality than we are."

"Fuck his morality. We're the ones who have to be brothers with these kids when he's long gone."

"Yeah," Backstreet muttered. "He's graduating in the spring. We're stuck with these kids for the next three years."

I offered no reply as we exited the courtyard and walked off into the night. Blake was right. Bishop and his ideology were creating mistakes that we would inherit.

SPRING
Sophomore Year

CHAPTER NINE

FRATERNITY RUSH

"These are the guys we want."

"These kids fucking suck," I said.

"Seriously," Moody agreed. "What the fuck is wrong with this year's freshman class?"

"All the good kids rushed in the fall," Mitchell answered. "That's how it always is."

"Yeah, Moody," Fish said, his freckled face lighting up with a grin, "that's why we got stuck with tools like you last spring."

Moody chuckled, but did not feel the need to protest. The brown-haired, blue-eyed alpha male knew his membership was highly valued by our brotherhood. He was intelligent, he was athletic, and he was sociable. And perhaps most important of all—he was a face guy.

"What about that kid in the black shirt?" Mitchell asked. "The one standing next to Mendez."

"Who?" Moody asked with a snort. "The fat kid?"

"Nah, right behind him. That tall guy talking to Lorie."

I stared out the window overlooking the crowded front porch deck and observed a tall, lanky kid with spiky dark hair. He was a good-looking young man who seemed confident and relaxed as he conversed with the girl.

"His name is Mike or Matt," I said. "He seemed like a cool guy when we did his interview, but he said he isn't interested in rushing. He's just tagging along with his two boys who're fucking tools."

"What about that big guy?" Fish asked. "Right over there in the white button-down."

"Hell no," Mitchell said, his hand absently rubbing his

brown goatee.

"Hell no," Moody repeated. "He's some kind of power lifter, but his receding hairline is terrible from all the steroids he must be doing."

My eyes continued to scan over the crowd, searching for possible candidates. I saw a good-looking pair of young men dressed in blue jeans and untucked button-downs.

"What about those two kids from Smith Hall?" I asked my brothers. "The guys Rowdy and Mendez interviewed tonight."

Moody shrugged. "When I talked to them, they weren't sure they wanted to join a fraternity, but they're gonna stick around and come to the after-party."

"Good," Mitchell said. "If they're willing to stick around here instead of going to other houses, then they're definitely interested. Let's get them drunk as hell tonight and introduce them to as many girls as possible."

Fish nodded and asked, "What do you guys think about that one kid the older brothers keep pushing for?"

Mitchell smirked. "Pruitt's friend from High School?"

"Yeah."

"That kid is fucking lame. The rednecks just want some new blood to join their clique and suck their dicks."

"Fuck the older brothers," Moody said bitterly. "I *don't* want him just because they *do* want him."

I chuckled with a wide smile spread across my face. It was the first semester the younger brothers were in charge of Rush. Mitchell was the Rush Chairman and he was fully enforcing the elitist recruitment strategy of quality over quantity. Our strict standards were not being welcomed by the older brothers because we were rejecting many of the guys they wanted to be offered rush bids.

Fish snickered and pointed. "Look, look, look! Jacob is axing that fat kid with glasses."

"Bout time," Mitchell snorted. "That fucking turd has

been hanging out all night, hoping we'll give his fat ass a bid."

We silently watched Jacob escort the unwanted kid away from the large crowd of brothers, girls, and rushees on the deck. Jacob was a tall, red-haired brother with the reputation of a heavy drinker who freely spoke his mind. He was also known for being someone who did not shy away from confrontation, a trait he demonstrated one afternoon when he beat the shit out of some kid on the front staircase of Strozier Library. Anybody can fight drunk, but fighting on campus in the middle of a sober afternoon took balls. Jacob was thus the perfect candidate to fulfill the role of the Axe, a Rush duty that required him to blackball unwanted rushees.

Watching Jacob escort the rushee away from our house reminded me of the ugly nature of fraternities. I could not hear what my brother said to the kid, but knew it was probably something like: "Sorry, this is just not the right place for you. You need to leave."

The fat kid's shoulders slumped with shame as he walked away from our house. Jacob turned around, glanced up at the window, and gave us two middle fingers.

"Asshole," Moody chuckled.

"The biggest," Fish agreed.

I joined in the laughter of my friends, but my head shook in sympathy for the banished rushee.

"Hey, Mitchell," I asked, "weren't you the Axe last semester?"

"Yeah."

"How do you guys do that shit? I'd feel like a dick telling them to leave."

Mitchell snorted. "Sure, Bryce. You feel bad about telling people to their face they're not wanted, but you have no problem punching people in the face."

A sly smile formed on my lips. "Point taken. But still…" I gave my friend a small shrug. "Somehow it seems different. The kids I punch deserve that shit. Most of them anyways…"

Mitchell chuckled. "*Most* of them."

"You gotta axe kids like that," Moody declared frankly. "Toolbag rushees hanging around here makes us look bad."

No one argued. With nearly twenty fraternities vying for new recruits, Rush Week was a highly competitive process that demanded ruthless discrimination.

"Yo, here we go," Fish said keenly with his eyes staring out the window. "Those two rugby players from last night are back. These guys are studs."

We all looked at the sidewalk entrance where Diego was greeting two young men. It was always smart to put someone in the greeter position that rushees would instantly respect. In other words, it was a face-guy position that required affable social skills. Diego was perfect for the job with his laidback New York coolness and his handsome Italian looks. The two rushees shook Diego's hand and definitely seemed to be responding to his charm

"Hell yeah," I said. "These are definitely the guys we want."

"Alright, Bryce," Mitchell instructed, "you go talk to them for a few minutes and then bring them up to your living room. Moody and I'll be in there, ready to offer them bids."

"Cool. I'm on it."

I exited the apartment and descended the staircase to the Formal Living Room. When I stepped out the front door of my fraternity house, I bumped into the stout figure of Big Country. The handsome young man from Georgia was usually a cheerful kid, but tonight his voice was laced with bitterness.

"What the fuck, Bryce?" he asked. "Why hasn't my little brother been given a bid?"

I played stupid. "He hasn't been given one yet?"

"Nope."

"Has he been interviewed?"

Big Country nodded. "Rowdy and Rivera interviewed

him earlier tonight, but he shouldn't even have to be interviewed. He's a legacy. So why hasn't he been given a fucking bid yet?"

I anxiously rubbed the back of my shaved head. This was not a question I wanted to answer. Big Country's step-brother had recently transferred to FSU, but offering the quirky young man a rush bid had been strongly opposed by Mitchell, me, and the rest of the brothers serving on the Rush Committee. Sharing this harsh truth with Big Country was not something I had the heart to do.

"I don't know, man," I finally answered. "It's out of my hands. Talk to Mitchell about it."

Before he could reply, I wandered off to search the crowded deck for the rugby players. Several young women in tight jeans distracted me, but I eventually found the duo conversing with Blake and Backstreet. The latter saw me approach and stepped forward to greet me.

"*Bryce*," he whispered, "we need to give these kids a bid. Both of them got approved at the Rush meeting tonight when we went over their questioner sheets."

I nodded. "Yeah, we recognized them from upstairs. That's why I came down here. I'm about to take them up to Mitchell."

Backstreet flicked his tongue ring and said, "The girls at the door liked them. They wrote *Luke* and *Tom* on their nametags with huge bubble letters."

I grinned. "That code is genius. I've been ignoring every rushee I see with his name written in tiny letters."

We turned around to face Blake and the rushees and I sized up the two potential recruits. Luke was about 6ft. tall with dark hair he wore in a short fade. His roommate Tom was also six feet tall, but his crew-cut blonde hair and fair complexion contrasted sharply with Luke's darker features. They were both good-looking and muscular.

"Hey, Bryce," Blake asked, "do you remember Luke

and Tom?"

"Yeah, the rugby players, right?"

The two young men nodded and I extended a firm handshake to both of them.

"What's going on, Luke? Good to see you again, Tom."

"What's up, Darren?" Luke replied.

"How you doing, Darren?" Tom asked.

"I'm glad you boys came back," I said with a friendly smile. "Did you get a chance to stop by any of the other houses?"

"Yeah," Luke replied, "we saw a few last night and some more tonight."

Tom grinned. "The Sigmas had the Hooters Girls over there serving wings."

Blake immediately set his Pepsi down on the deck railing and gave us a big smile.

"Hell yeah," he said jokingly. "I'm gonna go there right now and pretend I'm rushing so I can eat wings and look at big titties."

The rushees laughed and I made a mental note to tell Mitchell about the Sigma Rush strategy.

Backstreet decided to share a story with the rushees about banging out a Hooters girl. I had never heard the story before which meant it could have been bullshit, but Luke and Tom seemed to be responding to his macho charisma. It was time to extend the invitation.

"Do you two want to come upstairs?" I asked. "There are some brothers up there who'd like to speak with you."

"Definitely," Tom answered.

"Sure," Luke replied with a knowing smile of what this likely meant.

I nodded towards the house. "Follow me."

The rugby players trailed me into the house and up into my apartment. It was your typical frat pad—wooden paddles hung on the wall, empty liquor bottles stood on top of the entertainment center, and a fish tank that had not been cleaned in months sat in the corner. There was an electric guitar mounted on the wall and next to it hung a poster of *Korn* and the deceased rapper Tupac Shakur using middle fingers to flip-off the camera. Mitchell and Moody were sitting on the couch, the lights were dimmed, and there were candles lit on the coffee table to signify the ceremonial status of what was about to happen next.

"What's going on, guys?" Moody asked.

Mitchell smiled warmly. "What's up, boys?"

Both brothers were dressed in black slacks and button-down dress shirts with the sleeves rolled up. They rose from the couch to shake hands with the rushees before inviting the young men to sit on the adjacent couch. Luke and Tom took a seat, and sensing the seriousness of the moment, they sat forward with elbows resting on their knees.

The Rush Chairman spoke first. "I'll get right to the point, gentlemen. The reason we invited you up here tonight is because we want to offer you a bid."

Moody smoothly followed. "You have all the qualities we're looking for in a pledge. You're intelligent, athletic, sociable—and you guys are studs."

Mitchell spoke again. "Rowdy and I did your interviews last night and thought highly of both of you. We would've offered you a bid, but we don't like to give out bids on the first night. But you're definitely the kind of guys we're looking for to become brothers of Upsilon."

He reached out to the coffee table and picked up one of two small golden pins engraved with the Greek letter of Upsilon.

"I have these pledge pins for you," Mitchell continued, "and if you accept them, we'll take you downstairs and put them on you in front of the brotherhood."

Moody hedged the offer. "You don't have to accept your bid tonight and it's good all week long, but if you want to join Upsilon, then we can make you pledges right now."

The two rushees glanced at each other and nodded their heads. Dark-haired Luke spoke first.

"We've been to other fraternity houses and we think this is the best brotherhood we've seen."

My eyebrows arched in amusement. If this was truly their opinion, then the two rushees must have made the same mistake I made as a freshman in failing to visit many houses.

Blond-haired Tom nodded his head. "You guys seem like the most laidback, most diverse group of guys on campus. We were turned off by all the clones we saw at the other fraternity houses."

"Yeah," Mitchell chuckled. "They look, talk, and dress the exact same."

"We also love sports," Luke said and shifted his gaze to the biceps I was showing off in a tight polo. "Athletics seem to be real big around here."

"Definitely," Moody replied. "And we play to win. If you guys are good, you'll start."

Mitchell glanced towards me. "Bryce, you got anything to add, big man?"

I flashed my most charming smile at the pledges and said what every fraternity member says during Rush Week.

"The only thing you guys need to know about Upsilon is that we party harder than any other fraternity and we pull the best-looking girls on campus."

Our sales pitch worked. Tom and Luke accepted their bids and we took the young men downstairs one at a time to formally introduce them as new members of Upsilon. I went first with a cow bell, striking it with a wooden drumstick as I marched down the stairs and out the front door. Luke followed right behind me and the Rush Chairman trailed behind him. When I reached the center of the deck, I stopped and turned around to face the excited freshman.

Mitchell stuck the pledge pin in Luke's shirt, raised his

fist above the young man's head, and yelled, "Hooooooooo!"

A rowdy pack of brothers swarmed the new pledge, threw their hands up above his head, and proceeded to do the Upsilon tribal chant:

> *Highty tighty God almighty,*
> *who the hell are we?*
> *We're the men of Upsilon,*
> *the best fraternity!*
> *Hoooooo!*

CHAPTER TEN

PLEDGE MARSHALL

"That's all hazing really is."

The telephone rang.

"Hello?"

"Yo, this is Bryce. You've just been called in, motherfucker." Click.

The pledge hung up the phone and slowly turned to face his roommate. "Shit, dude. We just got called in."

"Fuck! Start calling them!"

He proceeded to call three of his pledge brothers who would thereafter call three of their pledge brothers and so on until the entire pledge class was made aware that they needed to be at the fraternity house in less than ten minutes. Those with cars took the stairway down to their dormitory parking lots and sped over to the fraternity house, picking up a few pledge brothers along the way. Those without cars sprinted across campus like their lives depended on it.

As we waited for the pledges to arrive, I stood with Moody and Blake in the Upsilon courtyard with twenty brothers. Blake and I wore camouflage pants and black wife beaters. Other brothers were dressed in military fatigues, combat boots, and even ski masks. Nearly everyone was armed with a Mag-Lite flashlight.

I pulled hard on a cigarette and exhaled a cloud of smoke. It was my first hazing session as Pledge Marshall and I was looking forward to exercising my power.

"Glenn better not show up," Blake said.

"You know he will," I replied. "I tried to keep tonight a secret, but that guy *always* shows up for Flashlight in the Corner."

"You're the Pledge Marshall," Moody said. "Why don't you just tell him to leave?"

"Because I don't believe I have the right to tell any brother not to haze. If he goes overboard with what he says or he tries to get physical, then yeah, but otherwise..." I shrugged my shoulders. "He's a brother and he's earned the right to haze."

Blake had a large pinch of dip tucked under his lip. He spit tobacco to the courtyard and snorted in amusement.

"Glenn get physical?" he repeated. "That crooked tooth motherfucker ain't getting physical with nobody. The last time he tried to get physical was that Halloween brawl when he got knocked the fuck out."

I snorted. "He tried to spread a rumor he was punched with brass knuckles."

Moody and Blake laughed.

"You know what?" I said thoughtfully. "That's probably why he loves Flashlight in the Corner so much. He can get in the faces of all the alpha male pledges and talk shit to them without getting his ass kicked."

"Hell yeah," Blake agreed. "He'd never try that shit in the real world because he'd get fucked up for running his bitch mouth."

Moody nodded. "Hazing pledges is the one time a guy like that will ever hold power over guys like us."

Blake spit tobacco and said, "I hated being hazed by a kids like Glenn who don't even come around here anymore. You gotta just stand there and get yelled at by some goofball you've never seen before."

I chuckled. "It's a good life lesson in self-control."

"That's all hazing really is," Moody said.

Blake shook his head. "Nah, yo...that shit is a tool to get rid of the kids you don't want."

"Yeah, but for guys like us, being hazed is about learning to put up with bullshit and walk away." Moody chuckled, and added, "I don't know how you two aggressive fucks survived it."

Blake grinned. "We were drunk as shit most of the time. I can barely remember our Call-Ins now."

Moody's eyebrows arched in amusement. "I remember last fall when you guys would get called in. The rest of the 706 Crew would just stay in your dorm room and finish off the beer."

"Assholes," Blake replied.

I grinned at Blake. "That's okay. I remember last spring when we used to drink in our dorm room before heading over to the house to haze Moody."

Blake laughed. "Tah ha. Hell yeah. I loved that shit."

Moody chuckled and asked, "So how are the pledge meetings going this semester?"

I pulled a drag and shrugged. "Good. Same old shit. I'm making them memorize the creed, our fraternity colors, and the founding fathers. Patterson got the weekly *I fucked a fat chick award* and Horton got the *dumb ass* award for passing out in his dorm bathroom."

Moody nodded. "Are you gonna teach them anything different this year?"

"Yeah. Group responsibility. That everything they do as individuals affects the reputation of our brotherhood. I told them the Pi story, about why those guys got kicked off campus."

"That shit was fucked up," Blake said and spit tobacco.

"What's the Pi story?" Moody asked.

"Seriously?" I replied, flicking my cigarette into the courtyard. "You've never heard this one? Man, that shit *was* fucked up."

"So what happened?"

"Back in the late eighties, some Pi brothers drugged a girl with Roofies and then ran a train on her while she was passed out. When they were done, they took some magic markers and wrote our fraternity letters all over her naked body and then left her on our doorstep."

Moody's blue eyes widened. "Holy fuck. That's just wrong."

"Fucking assholes," Blake said and spit tobacco. "But at least she knew who did that shit to her and got them all arrested. Their whole fucking fraternity got kicked off campus."

"Group responsibility," I said again. "Everything we do as individuals affects the reputation of our brotherhood."

"Hell yeah," Blake agreed.

I watched him spit tobacco and said, "Yo, nigga…give me some of that dip."

Blake handed me the mint-flavored Skoal and I threw in a fat pinch. When I handed the small container back to him, he shook his head and spit tobacco.

"I swear to fucking god," he said, "Glenn better not show up."

"He probably will," I replied and spit tobacco. "But I got the solution if he does."

"What?"

"The Monster."

The three of us laughed wickedly.

CHAPTER ELEVEN

ICE-CREAM SOCIAL

"Creed Speak!"

"Here come some more," Big Country said. "They look more excited than scared."

"Yup," Mitchell replied. "They'll know better next time. This is their first Ice-Cream Social."

"Mine too," grinned the large freshman. "At least as a brother."

"You're gonna love hazing," Mitchell said with a knowing chuckle. "It's the best part of being in a fraternity."

"Nah, dude. The best part is all the pussy I'm getting."

"Yeah...that too."

"Bro, I fucked this one girl doggy-style last night for like two hours straight. I was so drunk I couldn't cum."

"Did you nut?"

"Yeah, eventually. She had this picture of her mom and her little sister next to the bed. I stared at that shit and thought about cumming on their faces."

"You're a sick fuck."

"Yup."

Mitchell chuckled. "Look. Here comes the rest of em."

The two brothers watched the final group of pledges approach the back of the Upsilon house. Most of the young men were huffing and puffing from their hectic flight across campus.

"Line up," Mitchell commanded. "Line the fuck up."

The pledges formed in a line facing their Assistant Pledge Marshall. They were all dressed in blue jeans and white t-shirts and their faces revealed a variety of emotions. Some were scared. Some were drunk. Some looked like they had just rolled out of bed.

Mitchell stared down at his watch. "It's ten minutes past one, gentlemen. Congratulations. You made it on time."

He marched up and down the line, inspecting the pledges like a drill sergeant. Mitchell was wearing camouflage pants and a tight black t-shirt, and when he spoke, it was with the smug, arrogant tone of voice you'd expect from a young man who wanted to be a cop.

"Pledges," he said, "you will not speak tonight unless you're spoken to. You will not move unless you're told to move. You will not breathe unless you're told to breathe."

All the pledges remained silent with their eyes straight forward. The cocky ones were smiling and the scared ones seemed to be holding their breaths. The inebriated appeared to be having trouble standing.

"When I give the order," Mitchell said, "you're gonna follow Big Country up the stairs, through the courtyard, and into the basement bathroom. Do you understand?"

The "Yes, Sirs" that followed were spoken at multiple intervals, but by the end of the semester, their voices would speak as one.

Mitchell nodded in satisfaction and turned to face the stout figure of Big Country who looked all too eager to haze.

"Take them up, Big Country!"

The tall freshman charged up the concrete staircase and the pledges followed him in a single file line. They ran up the stairs, through the hallway, down another staircase, and through the empty courtyard. When they entered the dark basement, they were shoved into the bathroom. A strobe light lit up the room and a handful of brothers wearing camouflage were waiting inside. The verbal lashing began almost immediately.

"You fucking pledges suck ass!"

"You're the worst fucking pledge class I've ever seen!"

"Don't fucking eyeball me, boy! I'll skullfuck you!"

"Do you think you deserve to be here?"

"You don't, bitch! You fucking don't!"

"Why the fuck would I want to call you my brother?"

"Creed Speak!"

The pledges recited the Upsilon Creed like druids chanting an ancient prayer. Brothers screamed louder and their words got uglier.

"Keep your eyes down, you fucking cunt!"

"What the fuck is wrong with you, bitch? Don't stutter my creed."

"Eyes down, motherfucker. Eyes down!"

"Stand up straight, you fat face fuck!"

"I said don't look at me! I'll kill your faggot ass!"

"Creed Speak!"

It always got extremely hot in the small, damp bathroom and it was not long before both pledges and brothers were sweating profusely. After five minutes of this verbal abuse, the pledges were herded into the main chamber of the basement. Plated weights and dumbbells were waiting on the ground.

"Pick up a weight," I said to the pledges from the center of the room. "Pick it up and hold it to your chest.

Each of the pledges picked up one the weights. Some of them made the mistake of racing to pick up a lighter load.

I smiled. "We don't take shortcuts here, gentlemen. If you just picked up a ten pound weight, I want you to switch with someone who picked up a fifteen or twenty pounder."

Some groaned and some smiled at the result of this exchange. None of the young men would be smiling soon.

"Alright, on the ground, on your fucking backs!"

The pledges spread out and lay down on the bare basement floor.

"Now extend the weight behind your head as far as you can."

The pledges stretched out their arms, plates and

dumbbells scraping the ground.

"Now straight leg lift your legs to the sky."

Legs came up.

"Now straight arm lift the weight."

Arms came up and the bodies of the pledges resembled the letter U.

"Now lower them both to the ground."

Legs came down and arms came down.

"Good," I said. "Now this time when I say up, I want you to lift the weight and your legs at the same time. And when I say down, I want you to call out the count."

A few tense seconds passed before I shouted, "Up!"

Arms and legs came up.

"Down!"

"One!" shouted the pledges.

"Up! Down!"

"Two!" shouted the pledges.

"Up! Down!"

"Three!"

And so it began. I forced the pledges to perform this demanding exercise over and over again. Those who faltered were screamed at by drunk brothers who blinded the young men with flashlights and poured beer on their faces. Mitchell and a few brothers were on their hands and knees, snarling and cussing in the faces of the kids they didn't like. When the pledges finally reached fifty, I let them climb to their feet and take a breather, but my mercy would be short-lived.

"Alright, pledges!" I yelled. "Take your weights to the wall and sit on air."

A few of the pledges hesitated but followed the lead of their pledge brothers who were familiar with the endurance exercise known as wall sits. The young men put their backs to the wall and sat down on air, holding themselves aloft with their leg muscles.

"Patterson, you dumb shit!" Blake screamed. "Don't

put your weight down. Pick that shit back up!"

The husky, corn-fed Nebraskan quickly picked up his twenty pound weight and resumed his position on the wall. Sweat was already trickling down his chubby cheeks.

"Now lift your arms straight out!" I yelled. "Up!"

The pledges held the weights out in front of them.

"Creed Speak!" I screamed.

The young men recited the Upsilon Creed as their shoulders strained against the law of gravity.

"Down!" I screamed. "Up! Creed Speak!"

They recited the creed many times over. Those who faltered were cursed at and threatened by drunk brothers itching for any excuse to verbally abuse the young men.

"Fuck you, pledge!"

"Is that all you got?"

"Why the fuck would I want you for a brother!"

"Don't you have any heart!"

"You're fucking weak, bitch! You're fucking weak!"

A spiky-haired pledge actually made the fatal mistake of dropping his weight. Punishment was administered by Rowdy who shook up a beer bottle and placed his thumb over the mouth of the container so that foaming alcohol sprayed up into the kid's eyes.

"What the hell?" the pledge screamed in pain.

"Fuck you, bitch boy!" Rowdy yelled. "Alphabet Speak!"

The entire pledge class recited the Greek alphabet.

"Creed Speak!" Rowdy snarled.

As they chanted the creed, legs started shaking and plated weights started wobbling. I nodded in satisfaction. This was enough for now. There was no reason to mentally push them beyond their physical capacities because tonight wasn't about will power. It was about self-control.

"Down!" I yelled. "Now rack your weights in the weight room and get in the fucking bathroom!"

A sober brother followed them in there to perform the good cop duty of measuring their emotional stability. Most young men endured hazing without suffering anything more than indignation and physical exhaustion, but there were always a few thin-skinned pledges who had never been subjected to exhaustive physical exercise or the unpleasant experience of someone cussing in their faces. These sorts would always bear watching. Sheltered youths with crybaby potential were not exactly coddled, but with FSU administration always breathing down our necks, we had to be wary of doing something to a pledge that might cause him to report our prohibited hazing activities to IFC.

When the good cop informed me that all the pledges seemed mentally stable, it was time to begin Flashlight in the Corner. The pledges were brought out of the bathroom one at time and forced to stand in a corner. With his back to the wall, the young man faced the entire assembly of drunk bothers who took turns blinding the pledge with a flashlight while yelling at him to Creed Speak, answer fraternity trivia, or account for a recent discourtesy towards a brother. Some of these verbal lashings were comical. Others were serious.

"What the fuck is wrong with you?" Backstreet screamed in the face of a pledge. "I saw you at our soccer games and you weren't making enough noise! Why the fuck didn't you cheer?"

"I did, Sir!"

"Fuck you, pledge! Are you calling me a liar?"

"No, Sir."

"You weren't fucking cheering and you disrespected your Pledge Marshall who used his own money to get you drunk before the game." Backstreet's mouth was now just inches away from the pledge's face. He flicked his tongue ring and yelled, "Bryce gets you drunk and you can't even scream at the other team? What the fuck! Were you scared of them? Are you some kind of pussy?"

"No, Sir, I—"

"Shut the fuck up!" Backstreet screamed. "I don't want to hear your bullshit excuses! Creed Speak!"

The next pledge put in the corner was ordered to recite the Upsilon Creed. He got about halfway through the recitation before he began to stumble over his words. Blake charged at the pledge and slammed his open palm against the wall, inches away from the kid's head.

"What the fuck is wrong with you?" he yelled. "I took you guys to Strozier Library yesterday for study hours and you can't even memorize the creed of the fraternity you want to join? Why the fuck haven't you learned our creed?"

The skinny pledge looked scared. "I-I-I'm taking a lot of hard classes. I don't have as much time as I'd like to—"

Blake slammed his hand against the wall again. "Shut the fuck up! I saw your ass shooting pool yesterday in the basement and I saw you hanging out in Mendez's room, watching TV! Don't tell me you don't have time! Make time! Learn my creed or get the fuck out of my fraternity!"

Another pledge was put into the corner and he failed to name the founding fathers of Upsilon, something I had told the pledges to memorize a few days ago during their weekly pledge meeting. I approached the young man with a hardbound copy of the Upsilon manual in my hand. My head shook with disappointment.

"Stanley," I said, "I gave you a copy of this manual to learn are founding fathers, to learn our colors, and to learn our ideals. We teach you these things to build unity through an appreciation of our shared traditions."

I slammed the book against the wall so hard that its spine was ripped open and pages fluttered to the ground.

"Fuck you!" I snarled. "Fuck you! That's what you're telling me you feel about my fraternity. I swear to fucking god, you better get your shit together or we'll kick you the fuck out of here. If you shit on my fraternity, I'll shit on you!"

Some of the pledges were hazed for specific reasons, but more often than not, a brother would curse and scream at a pledge for no reason at all. It was fun to haze. We all enjoyed it without regret. It had been done to us and it had been done to the guys who did it to us. Hazing united young men in a way that no other activity could—it made us work for our brotherhood and it got rid of the guys who weren't serious about joining.

One brother did have a more specific purpose in his hazing—alleviating his personal inadequacies. Glenn showed up to the hazing session armed with the biggest Mag-Lite flashlight I had ever seen. The feverish way he held it reminded me of those small guys you see driving around in huge trucks to satisfy their Napoleon Complex. Glenn definitely had self-confidence issues which were clearly reflected in the way he hazed. The skinny older brother never yelled. Instead, he sneered out vicious words of condescension that seemed to slither off his crooked teeth. When he cursed and jeered at the pledges, his brown eyes became slits behind his glasses and I could see the angry kid he was in High School who was picked last in gym class and was never looked at twice by girls. The message he brought tonight was the same message he always brought.

"Fuck you, pledge. Do you think you're better than me? Are you fucking smiling? Do you think you belong here?" Do you think you're better than me? You're not! You need to show me some respect or I'm not letting you into *my* fraternity! Do you think you're better than me? Huh? Do you? Fuck you, pledge!"

My head shook with sympathy for the alpha male pledges that Glenn felt the need to single out. What some of my bothers failed to understand is that there is a huge difference between pledges respecting you and respecting your power. Guys like Glenn constantly abused their status as brothers by demanding a deferential form of reverence from our pledges that they never rightfully earned.

The final pledge to be put in the corner was Alex and Glenn was particularly eager to haze him. This concerned because I knew the pledge to be a violent prone young man.

"Fuck you," sneered the older brother, his mouth and drunk breath mere inches from the pledge's face. "Do you think you're better than me? Do you think you're better than me? You're nothing, man. You're fucking nothing."

Alex's brown eyes stared fiercely over Glenn's shoulder and his nostrils flared in anger.

"Fuck you, pledge." Glenn sneered. "Fuck you. If you don't shape up, I'll never let you in my fraternity. Do you think you're better than me? You're nothing, pledge, and you'll always be nothing. I'll beat the shit out of you."

Alex's fists knuckled up. It was time to intervene. I shouldered Glenn out of the way, grabbed the pledge by both of his arms, and guided him away from the pack of brothers.

"Alex," I said firmly, "go into the weight room right fucking now."

Mitchell had already gathered up the other pledges in the bathroom and was escorting them into the weight room. Brothers that tried to follow us into the workout facility were denied access by Blake.

"Stay out," he said. "The Call-In is over. Bryce wants to talk to his pledges alone."

My roommate shut the doors and I stared at the faces of my pledges. Some looked tired, some looked angry, and some looked distressed, but all of them looked like they wanted to go home.

I spoke my words calmly and candidly, like a devoted big brother to his younger siblings.

"I've been where you are before. Some of you had it rough tonight. There were guys out there hazing you that you may not like, respect, or even know. You had to deal with their bullshit and you had to deal with their inadequacies. But that's life, gentlemen."

Mitchell nodded. "Bryce is right, guys. In any large organization, you're gonna have to deal with people you don't like and you don't respect and you're gonna have to put up with their bullshit."

I looked around the room and said, "Some of the hazing tonight you probably earned. When we tell you to learn something, you need to learn it. Knowing the history of Upsilon gives us unity. And being hazed serves its own purpose. It gets rid of the guys who don't really care about being here and it gets rid of the guys who don't *deserve* to be here."

My gaze scanned over the pledges again. Some of their faces had softened. Others like Alex remained rigid with anger.

I smiled. "But I don't want you guys to feel like punching bags, so we're gonna try something a little different tonight. Being hazed in that corner out there was a lesson in self-control. But that's over. What goes on in here right now is about *losing* control. I'm gonna give you a chance to release your frustration and anger."

I flicked off the lights and Blake turned on the strobe light. The rapidly flashing machine lit up the large mirrors on the wall and this illuminated the room like a diabolical séance.

"Tonight..." I said with a peculiar tone, "tonight I'm gonna give you a chance to show us the Monster."

Mitchell chuckled as he turned on the stereo and sadistic heavy metal started blasting. I moved behind the bench press and smiled wickedly.

"Who's first?" I yelled.

One by one, the pledges lay down on the bench and were screamed at to press out the weight for as many reps as they could. When they tried to rack the bar, we shoved it away and screamed at them louder.

"Fuck you! Get pissed!"

"Think about those brothers hazing you!"

"Think about how that made you feel!"

"Press that shit!'

"Hell yeah, motherfucker!"

"Get pissed off!"

"Dig deep!"

"Push, motherfucker!"

"Exhale when you press!"

"Come on, kid!"

"Is that all you got, bitch?"

"One more!"

"One more!"

"One more!"

"Yeah, motherfucker!"

"Show me the monster!'

"Show me the rage!"

"Feel that shit!"

At first it was just me and my two fraternity brothers screaming, but the pledges were soon caught up in the adrenaline surge and they too started yelling at one another.

"Come on, motherfucker!"

"Yeah, Taylor! Get some! Get some!"

"Get pissed! Get pissed!"

"Think about those guys hazing you!"

It was a fascinating thing to behold. Young men firing each other up and mentally pushing one another beyond their physical capacities. This was real unity—men stirring up their hostility and rage together.

I brought things to an end when Alex got so fired up he started punching the bench, growling and snarling like an animal.

"FUCK YOU!" he screamed. "FUCK YOU! FUCK YOU! FUCK YOU!"

Some of the pledges laughed, but I knew we had just tapped into something else, something deep, something buried in his past. This wasn't anger at being hazed. This was hatred. Pure hatred.

I knew this and I smiled. It was sickly pleasurable to beckon forth the demons of other young men.

CHAPTER TWELVE

POSITIVE REPRESENTATION

"Perception, man. It's all that matters."

"Fuck those bitches!" Moody cursed as he stormed into my living room.

Blake, Joey, and I looked up from the television in surprise.

"Did you hear what happened?" he asked. "The Thetas issued an unofficial apology and they're still giving us a free social, but they're not doing it with us."

"What do you mean?" Joey asked.

"They're gonna *pay* for us to do a social with another sorority."

I stared at my friend in disbelief. "Are you serious?"

"Yeah, I'm fucking serious."

"That's fucked up," Blake said.

I shook my head. "They can't do that. They spelled it out themselves—whichever fraternity has the most brothers show up to the basketball tournament gets a free social with them."

"Nope," Moody said and sat down on the couch. "Now they're saying the offer was to *pay* for the winner to do a social, but it doesn't have to be with them."

"Wow," Blake said. "That's degrading as hell. They'd rather pawn us off to some other sorority."

Moody sneered. "Fuck those bitches. Let's take their money and buy a new television for the basement." His eyes lowered to the coffee table and the large jug of water in front of me. "Is that yours?"

"Yeah," I replied. "It's got creatine in it though."

My friend shrugged and lifted the jug to his mouth.

I leaned back on the couch and clasped my hands behind my head. A bitter smirk had formed on my face.

"You know…" I said. "We should probably be grateful *this* is even gonna happen. If Carlo hadn't caught those girls at the check-in desk writing down fake names for the Rhos, we'd be getting jack shit."

Moody slammed the jug on the table. "Fuck them and fuck their gay ass basketball tournament!"

Joey was sitting next to me on the couch. He rubbed his pointy chin and said, "I still can't believe those girls tried to get away with that. They must really have a thing for the Rho brothers."

"Hell yeah," Blake agreed. "They all want to do that Old South date formal with those redneck motherfuckers."

I shook my head. "Nah, man, it's got nothing to do with the Rhos and everything to do with us. Doing a social with Upsilon would hurt their reputation. It's all about status and perception."

"It's bullshit is what it is," Moody replied.

"Man, this sucks," Joey said with a frown on his baby face. "I wanted to do a pajama party with those girls."

"Hell yeah," Blake said with a leering grin. "Or a lingerie party."

The front door swung open and the muscularly lean figure of Mitchell entered the room. He was wearing blue jeans, sneakers, and a green Philadelphia Eagles jacket that looked way too small for him.

"What up, fellas?" Mitchell said with a beaming smile. "Your boy just aced his first Criminology exam of the semester."

Blake burst out laughing. "Yo, where'd you get that coat? I ain't seen anybody where a Starter jacket since like seventh grade."

"Whatever," Mitchell replied. "I'm from Fort Lauderdale. I don't have a fucking Jersey wardrobe full of nice winter clothes."

Blake giggled like a little kid. "Tah ha. Look at that thing! I bet you haven't worn it since middle school."

"Fuck you, Blake!" Mitchell growled.

I gave my friend an upwards head nod. "Did you hear the latest and greatest about Theta?"

Mitchell snorted. "You mean about paying for us to do a social with another sorority? That's fucking weak. Did you guys hear what Carlo did this morning?"

"No," Blake replied. "What?"

"My friend in Theta told me that he ran into one of those check-in girls at Kinko's Copy Center and reamed her out about what happened."

"Great," Moody said, throwing his hands up in frustration. "That's all we fucking need."

Joey stood up from the couch and slung his book bag over his shoulder. "Later, guys," he said. "I gotta get to class."

Mitchell occupied the vacated seat and I shook my head at him in disbelief.

"No way," I said. "Carlo wouldn't do that. He might've said something to her at Kinko's, but he's too smart to be an asshole to her."

Blake nodded. "That bitch is just trying to deflect her own shit, make it seem like Carlo is the bad guy in all this."

Moody shrugged. "Does it really matter? If *that's* what she's saying, then *that's* what her sisters are gonna believe."

"Bitches," Mitchell said.

Moody looked at me. "Bryce, you're right, man. It's all about perception and status. We got a shitty reputation because of the fucknut older brothers and the shitty recruits they didn't want to blackball. *That's* why the Thetas don't want to do a social with us."

"Hell yeah," Blake grumbled. "We're being discriminated against because of the losers in our fraternity."

I nodded. "Discrimination rules the Greek world."

"That shit's everywhere, bro," Mitchell said. "Even inside fraternities. *We* do it. Look at what happened to McDonald. That guy was a brother for two years and was hazed like a pledge until he finally quit this place."

Mitchell reached for the water jug in front of me. All meatheads love to hydrate.

"There's creatine in there," I warned.

"Good," he replied and tilted the jug to his mouth.

Blake shrugged dismissively. "Yo, I'm glad we got rid of McDonald. That motherfucker lied to me during Rush Week. He told me Upsilon did socials with all the best sororities."

"Bro, sororities get rid of people too," Mitchell said. "Some Deltas I know got some girl to move out of the house by writing a bunch of fucked up rhymes on her mirror about how she needs to lose weight."

Blake chuckled. "That's funny."

I snorted. "That's kind of like what the Betas do when their pledges go through Initiation Week. They have to stand blindfolded on a table in their panties and some girl pretends to use a magic marker to circle all her fat spots."

Mitchell laughed. "Yo, those bitches love to haze. Their new girls have to wear granny panties during Initiation Week and they all have to walk around campus with quarters in their shoes."

Moody's thoughts were still on the Theta controversy. "I'm tired of dealing with this shit," he said. "The four of us are good-looking guys with great social skills. We should be leaders on this campus instead of getting discriminated against because of our fraternity."

"Hell yeah," Blake said. "I'm tired of people looking down on me because kids like Goldman wear Upsilon letters."

Moody nodded. "You remember last year when that girl Kelly told us she was attracted to us, but wouldn't date us because she'd be embarrassed if her sisters found out what fraternity we're in."

Blake laughed. "Yo, you gotta respect that kind of honesty."

I shrugged at Moody. "That shit pisses me off too, but I'm not any better. When I find out a girl is in a shitty sorority, I think less of her, even if she is hot."

"Yup," Mitchell said. "It's guilt by association."

I picked up the plastic water jug and carried it to the kitchen sink for a refill. As water poured into the container, I raised my voice to be heard.

"That shit goes way beyond the Greek Life. I see it in the club every night. It's what *The Scene* is all about. You're defined by the kind of people you associate with. If all of your boys are good-looking, popular guys, then girls are gonna like you more."

"You can see it in the gym too," Blake said. "If you're cool with all the big juicers, then dudes respect you more and want to be your friend.

Mitchell nodded. "It's the same with chicks. If you're a girl and all your friends have fake tits, more guys will talk to you and invite you to their parties."

I returned to the living room and said, "Perception, man. It's all that fucking matters."

Moody's lip curled. "And the perception of our fraternity sucks ass right now. So what do we do about it?"

I sat back down on the couch and placed the water jug on the coffee table. My gaze shifted around the room.

"I've been thinking a lot about this…and I think the solution is positive representation."

Blake's eyebrows scrunched together. "What the fuck is positive representation?"

"It means all our face guy brothers with leadership skills need to represent Upsilon whenever and wherever they can. It means meathead brothers sporting our letters in the gym. It means good-looking brothers going to Greek events.

It means cool brothers getting jobs at bars and nightclubs."

Mitchell summed up my thoughts nicely. "We start getting our name out there and have it associated with studs instead of toolbag brothers."

"Exactly," I said. "That's why I'm gonna take that girl Jenny to her hayride."

"Who's Jenny?" Moody asked.

"Some Theta I met at one of our after-parties. Cute girl, auburn hair, pointy little nose." I glanced towards my roommate. "Blake, you remember her. Backstreet tried to hook up with her and she denied his ass."

Blake laughed. "Tah ha! That was funny as hell. Isn't she kinda plump?"

I shrugged. "She's a Theta. We need to start building a better relationship with those girls. Bosworth and Griswold are going too."

"You should *definitely* go," Moody agreed.

"I think another good place to start would be for the four of us to do that charity event Dance Marathon." I turned to Blake. "You gotta do that shit, right?"

"Hell yeah," he grumbled. "The Standards Board is making me go because of my fight with Timmy."

I nodded and looked around the room. "All of us should do it. It's thirty-two hours on our feet, socializing with every fraternity and sorority on campus."

"That's a good idea," Mitchell said.

"No, it's not," Moody replied. "I don't want to stand on my feet for thirty-two fucking hours."

"Yo, that's a good idea," Blake said a little too eagerly. "Let's do that shit."

Moody smirked at Blake. "You just don't want to have to do it alone or with some brothers you don't like."

"Yup," Blake agreed with a guilty smile.

Mitchell sat forward on the couch. "No, Bryce is right. We need to do Dance Marathon. Suck it up, Moody. Do it for the good of the fraternity.

"Fine," he said grudgingly. "Positive representation."

CHAPTER THIRTEEN

BACK IN TOWN

Bullshitting on the bench.

I stood alone in the empty courtyard of the Upsilon House and it felt strange. The memories came flooding back—me and Blake, right where I was standing, having the time of our lives, getting wasted and acting like assholes with our fraternity brothers. I had only been gone six weeks, but so different was my life in Atlanta that these memories of laughter and revelry felt like haunting ghosts. It was hard to believe I was finally back.

"Darren!" a familiar voice exclaimed. "Are you back in town?"

I turned around and saw Bishop returning from class with a red book-bag slung over his shoulder.

"Yeah," I replied. "I'm gonna be passing in and out of town for the next couple of weeks."

We shook hands with smiles. The clean-cut, dark-haired young man seemed genuinely pleased to see me and it was good to see him too. Even after all the political battles we fought against one another in the past, Bishop was still a brother I liked and respected.

"So how've you been?" he asked. "How's the ankle doing?"

We both stared down at my grey walking cast. It looked like the mechanical leg of a robot.

"Better," I replied. "Much better. I should be out of this thing in a few a weeks. I'm just glad to finally be off the crutches."

Bishop nodded sympathetically and raised his eyes to scrutinize the rest of me. I was much smaller than the last time he saw me, but it was not my shrunken physique that Bishop commented on.

"Wow," he said, "that shaved head of yours has really grown out."

I chuckled. "Yeah, that's something I'm gonna take care of quick."

"Get Dave to do it. He just hooked me up yesterday. Probably my last college town fade before I graduate."

"Bryce!"

"Hell yeah, yo! Bryce!"

My gaze shifted to the black metal staircase mounted against the front building of the fraternity house where I saw Blake and Mitchell emerging from my old apartment.

"What's up, boys!" I screamed and threw my hands up in the air.

Blake and Mitchell came running down the stairway to greet me and Bishop faded away.

"Hell yeah!" Blake screamed again. "The wayward Flex Brother returns!"

I watched the two young men approach and measured them for any notable changes. Mitchell's chin goatee had grown in thicker and the tightness of his blue Upsilon t-shirt hinted that he might have put on a few pounds of muscle in my absence. Blake had definitely put on some size. My roommate's big brown arms looked bigger than ever and so did his lat spread. I also noticed he was wearing a pair of grey Adidas shorts that belonged to me.

The elated duo embraced me with handshakes and hugs before the clowning inevitably started up.

"Holy shit!" Mitchell laughed. "Take a look at this motherfucker's hair, bro!"

Blake stared down at my walking cast. "Nah, yo, look at that fucking moon boot! You gotta let me borrow that for Quarts on the Court. I could get mad ups in that thing."

"Seriously," Mitchell chuckled. "That thing looks like a

fucking cyborg leg!"

The playful banter of old friends felt good. I smiled and asked, "You boys are still doing Quarts on the Court?"

Blake nodded. "Yup. Every Friday. There's been a lot of girls coming now too."

"Bryce!" shouted a familiar voice.

I turned around and saw Dave walking up into the courtyard from the gravel parking lot. Clad in gym shorts and a sleeveless t-shirt that exposed a tribal tattoo on his right shoulder, the handsome, blonde-haired Floridian was still a cool-looking customer.

"What's up, man?" he asked with a smile.

"You tell me," I replied and pointed at my hair. "Does it look like I need a fade?"

My fraternity brother grinned. "You want to do it right now?"

"Please."

"Alright, let's do it," he said and shook my hand. "Meet me in the basement. I'll go grab the clippers."

The older brother walked off and my attention returned to Mitchell and Blake. It was now my turn to dish out the jokes.

"Nice shorts," I said to Blake. "Did you spend all your laundry money on steroids or something?"

Mitchell snorted. "Blake has been raiding your closet ever since you left, bro!"

"Hell yeah," Blake replied. "There's some good shit in there for me to wear."

"You boys are looking big!" I said and grabbed Mitchell's bicep. "What is that in there? NO2 or D-bol?"

The meathead duo stood up straighter and puffed out their chests. Blake nodded with the cockiness of a young man whose efforts in the weight room have produced results.

"We've been training real hard," he said. "Sometimes Tadd lifts with us too."

My eyebrows arched. "You boys are lifting with Big Tadd now? You definitely aren't bullshitting on the bench!"

"Hell nah!" Mitchell exclaimed with a laugh.

I shot Blake a look and we both joined in the laughter. Bullshitting on the bench meant someone was not getting the job done in the gym, but unbeknownst to Mitchell, this expression had originally been about his macho tendency to rack more weight on the bar than he could handle.

Dave emerged from his upstairs apartment with clippers in one hand and a barber's cutting cape in the other.

"So what's up?" I asked my two friends. "Where you boys at now?"

"Bro, I gotta take off," Mitchell replied. "I got some reading to do for a test tomorrow, but I'll drop by your room afterwards. It's great to have you back."

"It's great to be back," I replied and shook my friend's hand again. "I missed you fuckers."

Mitchell began walking towards the parking lot and Blake called out after him.

"Hey, Vader! Don't forget to bring me that DMX CD tomorrow!"

"Aight!" he replied and walked off.

Three minutes later, I was sitting on a barstool in the basement and Dave was cutting my hair. He ran a two on top and faded up the sides from a zero. Blake smiled when the hair started coming off.

"There we go," he said. "There's the *old* Bryce!"

My fraternity brothers Rowdy and Jacob were also watching the barber at work.

"Dave, where'd you learn to cut hair?" Jacob asked.

"I don't know," Dave shrugged. "It's just something I picked up in the dorms when I was a freshman."

"Dave's got skills," I attested. "He even cuts his dad's hair."

"Oh yeah?" Rowdy chuckled. "Is that why he gets laid

every time he comes into town?"

We all laughed. Dave's father had a well-earned playboy reputation.

"My old man looks young," Dave answered. "And when I give him a fade, he looks *real* young."

Jacob grinned. "That's the only reason I want kids—so I can come visit my sons in college and bang out all the little sluts they know."

"Sick fuck," Dave accused with a laugh.

"Yo, I want like ten sons," Blake claimed. "I'm gonna build a fucking army."

"An army of Blakes?" I asked. "That's a fucking scary thought."

"Hell yeah, yo!" Blake growled and flexed his muscles.

Rowdy grinned like a shark. "The only reason I want kids is so I can fuck my daughter's friends. Sleepovers will be a *must* at my household."

I snorted. "There's actually this guy in my parents' neighborhood that divorced his wife and married his eighteen-year-old daughter's best friend. No lie."

"*That's* how you do it!" Jacob chuckled. "You gotta ditch that first wife and go back for a younger one."

"Yup," Dave agreed. "The first one you make babies with. The second and third wife you keep on the pill so they maintain that youthful physique."

We all laughed like the college assholes we were.

"Yo, Bryce," Rowdy asked, "do you want to go to COURSE 701 tonight and drink pitchers? Backstreet should be working."

"Yeah, maybe...but I gotta spend some time with Allison first. Getting laid is definitely more of a priority than hanging out with you boys and the king of the Meat Locker."

My friends laughed and I recalled an incident that had occurred in my absence involving Backstreet and Blake.

"So, Blake," I asked, "what the fuck really happened

between you and Backstreet when I was gone?"

All the young men chuckled and Blake gave me a dismissive shrug.

"Whateva, yo," he answered. "We got into an argument outside his apartment. That drunk motherfucker started punching out all his window panels, cursing at me and shit. Glass was shattering in my face, so I went up to our kitchen and grabbed some knives."

My eyes widened. This was a part of the story Blake had conveniently left out of our phone conversation a few weeks ago.

"What the fuck did you do with those?" I asked.

"Whateva, yo," he said with another shrug. "That asshole came outside to look at the window and I started throwing blades at him from the stairs."

My jaw dropped and my friends laughed at my stunned facial reaction. This story had obviously been well circulated among the brotherhood.

"Did you hit him?" I asked.

"Nah, yo…but I came close. And I almost hit Carlo. He was scared as shit. Kept screaming at me, calling me fucking crazy."

"Nigga, you are crazy, throwing knives at people. What the fuck were you thinking?"

"Fuck him!" Blake said with a snarl. "That's what I was thinking."

Jacob chuckled. "Didn't Backstreet have to go to the hospital because his hands were all cut up?"

"Yeah," Blake answered. "He got like ten stitches."

"But you guys are cool now?" I asked.

"Yeah, we're cool," Blake replied and gave me a sly grin. "And we still haze pledges together."

"The fucking wolf pack," I said with a short laugh. Blake's words reminded me that Hell Week was coming up and an evil smile crossed my face.

"So what's up with the pledges?" I asked.

Rowdy shrugged. "Most of them are good kids."

Blake nodded. "Except those two clowns Horton and Patterson. They come around whenever they feel like it and they hang out with the rednecks all the time."

Jacob snorted. "Horton and Patterson are the redneck brothers' little bitches."

"That's not a surprise," I replied. "Especially Horton."

My friends grunted in agreement. Horton had gone to High School with one of the rednecks named Pruitt. That the pledge was hanging out with the redneck crew was therefore to be expected, but I was irritated he felt like this association gave him the right to slack off on his pledge duties.

Jacob had even more disturbing news. "Did you hear those two dumb-asses got caught wearing letters on campus?"

"Shut the fuck up," I said in disbelief.

"Yeah, Bryce," Rowdy said, "it's true. They were both wearing Upsilon t-shirts."

"Those kids are the fucking worst," Blake hissed.

Even the cheery Dave was perturbed. He shook his head and said, "Never would've happened when I was a pledge. Our whole pledge class would've been blackballed."

Wearing letters was the privilege of brothers who had survived Hell Week. For pledges to wear letters before being initiated was therefore a slap in every brother's face. As their former Pledge Marshall, this behavior was particularly offensive to me.

"What'd Mitchell do about it?" I asked.

"Hazed them," Blake replied with a shrug.

"Fuck that. Put the word out. Bryce is back in town and we're having a Call-In *tonight.*"

"That's what I'm talking about!" Rowdy yelled. The blonde-haired young man dropped down into a muscular pose and comically grunted like an animal.

"Fuck going to COURSE 701," Jacob said. "We'll

bring beer over to your place. What time are you gonna call those little shits in?"

"Midnight," I replied sinisterly.

"You gonna tell Vader?" Blake asked.

"Fuck Mitchell! Those pledges know who their fucking daddy is!"

Jacob and Rowdy laughed, but Blake frowned in disapproval.

"Nah…" I said, "I should probably tell him, huh?"

"Yeah."

"Yo, what's the deal with Mitchell's new nickname?"

"What? Vader?" Blake shrugged. "I don't know. He's been pissed off all the time like Darth Vader using the power of the dark side and shit. He's a gloomy kid."

"He still bullshitting on the bench?"

Blake giggled like a little kid. "Hell yeah, yo!"

CHAPTER FOURTEEN

MY FUCKING LETTERS

"This is just a taste!"

"Fuck Horton and Patterson," Jacob said. "We should just blackball them."

"Isn't Patterson a legacy?" Joey asked.

"Yeah," I answered, "his dad was a brother. He built the fraternity house.

Jacob snorted. "He what?"

"Supposedly his pops was involved with the actual construction of the house."

"I don't give a shit," Rowdy said.

"Me neither," Blake snarled. "Fuck his dad, his mom, and his baby sister."

Jacob nodded. "He deserves what he gets tonight because he wore my letters on campus. Period."

"Fuck Horton!" shouted a drunk brother.

"Yeah!" Joey yelled comically. "Crucify him!"

The room erupted with laughter, but I slowly nodded my head and said, "Crucify both of them.

"All of them," Rowdy grunted. "I'm hazing the shit out of every single one of these kids tonight."

My living room was crowded with brothers eagerly anticipating a night of hazing. Some of the young men wore camouflage and I myself had thrown on my former Pledge Marshall gear of camouflage pants and a black wife beater. I also intended to wear combat boots which required me to strap up my injured ankle in a sophisticated ankle brace.

"Does your ankle still hurt?" Joey asked me.

I glanced up at my baby-faced roommate. He was wearing his standard outfit—faded blue jeans, running shoes, and a white Upsilon t-shirt. Joey was not dressed for hazing because he was not a brother who hazed, probably because he didn't have a mean bone in his lanky body.

"My ankle doesn't hurt right now," I replied, "but it might if I kick a pledge in the face tonight."

Brothers laughed wickedly and I continued to wrap the straps around my ankle.

"So, Joey," I taunted, "are *you* gonna haze tonight?"

"No…probably not."

"You fucking pussy!" exclaimed a brother.

"Don't be a bitch, Joey!" Blake yelled.

"Grab your sack!" urged another brother.

Rowdy flexed his arms and growled, "Haze these fucking kids for wearing our letters!"

Joey laughed at their wasted effort to pressure him into acting like the cruel kid he was not. Rebuke would not work on the indifferent brother, so I tried another approach.

"Come on, man," I pressed, "I'll just put you on good cop duty tonight. We need someone to coddle Horton and Patterson in case they start crying."

Again he shook his head. "Nope. I just wanna watch."

I shrugged and pressed him no further. Some guys just weren't meant for hazing. Others were. Glancing around the room, I was disappointed to see a few faces missing that should have definitely been present.

"Where the fuck is Moody and Rivera?" I asked.

Blake shrugged. "Moody and Klein don't come around much anymore. They got some hard classes this semester, exercise physiology stuff like chemistry."

"Pussies," I said with a smirk. "What about Rivera?"

"He's gone missing in action again," Rowdy answered.

"You mean he's back together with his lady?"

"Yeah."

I shook my head with displeasure. "That's bullshit, Rowdy. Do you remember how cool that guy was freshman year? Remember our road trip to Gainesville?"

Rowdy chuckled. "Fuck yeah. We were driving seventy miles per hour and he climbed out the window and spread himself flat on the roof, Evil Kinevil style."

"With a ski mask on!" I added.

"Craziest shit I've ever seen."

"Balls," I said. "Big ones. And then we broke into that UF fraternity house and went on a scavenger hunt for treasure. Wait—didn't you come with us?"

Rowdy grinned like a shark and held his right hand up for us to see the long scar on his palm.

"Paid a price too," he replied. "Cut my fucking hand on that broken window."

"Here ya go, Bryce," Blake said and tossed me his cell phone. "It's dialing."

I lifted the phone and listened to it ring three times before the jovial voice of Taylor picked up.

"Hello?" he answered.

"Yo, this is Bryce. I'm back in town and you just got called in motherfucker." Click.

My fraternity brothers howled with laughter. It was definitely going to be a miserable night for the pledges.

"Yo, put some music on," someone said.

Blake inserted a CD into the music player and the intro of *Korn's* song "Blind" began to hum from the speakers.

"Uh oh, Bryce," Blake warned. "Uh ohhh!!!"

"Fuck yeah," I grinned. "We need to rage out."

When the heavy metal started cranking, Blake and I slam danced around the room, grunting like beasts. Our brothers laughed and joined in the rowdiness. After taking so many weeks off from the gym, I felt small, but I was also starting to feel like the old Bryce again—the badass in the fraternity who swung his fist as often as his dick.

The Call-In was a cruel sixty minute hazing session of intimidation tactics and intense calisthenics. I doubted

Mitchell slacked off on the pledges in my absence, but I was taking no chances and acted like he did. When the young men arrived at the fraternity house, they were herded into basement and shoved into a strobe light bathroom where I hazed them with fury.

"Motherfucking pledges!" I screamed. "I heard you've been doing a half-ass job! That shit's not gonna fucking slide anymore!"

Stomping around the small room, I bumped and shoved pledges and snarled in their faces.

"I'm back and I'm here to stay! If you want to be a brother of this place, you're gonna have to earn that shit!"

Blake, Rowdy, and Jacob were also in the bathroom, bumping and shoving around the pledges.

"Fuck you, Chris!" Rowdy yelled. "Keep your fucking eyes down and shut the fuck up!"

"I fucking hate you!" Blake snarled. "I fucking hate all of you!"

"Bitch, I will kill your ass!" Jacob shouted in a pledge's face. "Don't ever fucking look at me again!"

I whirled on Horton and squared off with him face to face. The eyes of the timid young man immediately lowered.

"What the fuck is wrong with you, Horton? You're gonna fucking wear *my* letters on campus?"

I slammed my fist against the wall, inches from his floppy-haired head.

"MY FUCKING LETTERS!?!?! WHO THE FUCK ARE YOU TO WEAR MY FUCKING LETTERS!?!?! YOU HAVEN'T EARNED THE RIGHT TO BE CALLED MY BROTHER, YOU FUCKING BITCH!!!"

Blake and Rowdy were all over the pledge as soon as I backed off.

"Fuck you, Horton!" Blake snarled. "You fat piece of fucking shit! Do you think we want your chubby ass on campus wearing our letters? Fuck you!"

Rowdy poured beer all over the kid's head and screamed, "You don't deserve to wear my letters! None of you fucking do until you make it through Hell Week!"

"That's right!" I yelled. "And I blame the rest of you fucking pledges for letting this dumb fucker right here think it was okay to wear letters. His screw up is *your* screw up! Creed Speak!"

The pledges chanted the Upsilon Creed like druids and a similar treatment of insults and beer showerings was inflicted upon Patterson. Wearing our letters on campus deserved nothing short of cruelty.

After the bathroom hazing, we led the pledges out into the main chamber of the basement where dumbbells and plated weights waited for them on the floor. The pledges were then put through the most brutal hazing they had yet to endure in the form of intense muscle endurance exercises. Pushups, leg lifts, lateral raises, pushups, lateral raises, and more pushups. Brothers screamed at the young men, blinded them with flashlights, and poured beer all over them.

"You fucking goddamn pussies!"

"Keep doing pushups!"

"Nobody said to stop!"

"Up, motherfucker! Up!"

"You weak fucking bitches!"

"Why the fuck would I want to call you my brother?"

"Creed Speak!"

When the pledges were approaching complete exhaustion, I forced them to perform wall-sits as they held the weights straight out in front of their chests.

"This is just a taste!" I snarled. "This is just a little fucking taste of what waits for you in Hell Week! I'm gonna be here all week long to take personal care of you!"

Pledges grimaced, sweated, and grunted as they strained to hold their body weight in the air and hold the weights straight out in front of them.

"Hell Week, bitches! You will not eat, you will not sleep, and you sure as shit won't become brothers until you've proven you've got something to contribute to this fraternity! Creed Speak!"

The pledges recited the Upsilon Creed as their arms wobbled with fatigue.

"Down!" I screamed.

Arms lowered and pledges sighed with relief. They were all breathing heavy and sweat trickled down their faces.

"Look, gentlemen," I said severely, "this is just a sample of what to expect. If you don't think you can handle a week of this shit, then you need to seriously think about whether or not you should come back after tonight."

The young men were still holding themselves aloft against the wall and they definitely looked worn out, but there was something in their eyes I didn't like. It wasn't defiance as much as it was cockiness.

"I don't think you guys get it yet. I don't think you believe me how hard it's gonna be. I think you need another taste. What do you think, brothers?"

"Haze these fuckers!" Jacob snarled.

"Fuck these kids!" Blake screamed. "Just send them home and tell them never to come back!"

"Haze them!" yelled more brothers. "Haze em! Haze em! Haze em!"

A few of the pledges were starting to look scared now that they realized tonight's activities might not be over.

"On the fucking ground!" I screamed. "Lay on your backs and hold your weights over your heads!"

Pledges groaned and were slow to react.

"Get the fuck down, bitch!" Rowdy barked in Horton's pudgy face.

Blake grabbed another pledge off the wall and slung him to the ground.

"Get your ass down there!" he snarled.

The rest of the pledges were dropping to the ground now and rolling onto their backs.

"Up!" I yelled.

Legs and weights came up so that the bodies of the pledges resembled the letter U.

"Down!" I screamed.

"One!" shouted the pledges.

"Up! Down!"

"Two!"

"Up! Down!"

"Three!"

And so on and so on until even the strongest among them was groaning like a blood torn casualty on the battlefield.

"Alright, pledges!" I finally shouted. "Stand the fuck up!"

The young men struggled to rise. Their faces were flushed and their white t-shirts soaked with sweat and beer.

"I want you to take your weights back to the weight-room and then go outside."

The pledges obeyed and filed out the door. Jacob was waiting in the courtyard with the hose.

"It's time to cool down!" he sneered at them. "Each of you gets a shower!"

One by one, they were sprayed down and forced to walk home shivering, exhausted, and very much fearful about what lay ahead.

"Jesus Christ," I heard one pledge ask another, "what do you think Hell Week is gonna be like?"

"Hell," his friend mumbled. "Fucking hell."

CHAPTER FIFTEEN

KARMA

"Should we feel bad?"

"You again?" asked the orthopedic technician.

"Nope," I replied. "It's my boy this time."

Kevin turned from me to look at Blake. With his big black thumb jabbed in my direction, he said, "You hanging out with this guy, it's no wonder you're in here."

My roommate chuckled. "Yeah, he's a regular around here."

I nodded at the technician. "Blake, this is the guy who cast up my ankle after Desperado."

"I also did his hand last summer," Kevin said as he eyeballed Blake's swollen ankle. "So what'd *you* do to get in here?"

The injured young man looked at me, looked at Kevin, and shrugged. "I hazed a fucking pledge."

* * * * *

The pledge had been hazed seventeen hours earlier at the Upsilon House. It happened when Blake returned from his afternoon class and found me sitting on the stairway overlooking the fraternity house courtyard.

"Did the pledges wash our dishes?" Blake asked.

"Horton is in there right now."

"Fuck Horton."

"Yup. He was the last one here today."

Blake snorted. "That kid always shows up late so all the house chores are done by the time he gets here."

"I know. That's why I made sure he did all our fucking

dishes. What class are you coming from?"

"Spanish."

"Hablas Español?"

"Si, Señor. Muy bien."

"Is that tan girl from last semester in your class?"

"Michelle?"

I shrugged. "The one you hooked up with. Tan as hell, nice body, always calling people *nigga*."

Blake laughed. "Yeah, that's her. She sits next to me."

"Does she still talk like a hood rat or has she chilled out with that shit?"

He laughed again. "She's worse, yo. That girl tries so hard to be down."

"How's her body looking?"

"Good. Real good."

"I guess that's all that matters."

Blake grinned. "Yup."

The door behind us swung open and the chubby figure of Horton emerged from our apartment. His floppy blonde hair was neatly combed and he was wearing khakis and a white button-down with a tie. It was Thursday which meant all the pledges had to dress up.

"Did you finish the dishes?" I asked him.

"Yup."

"Did you dry them?"

"Yeah."

"Good work, pledge."

"What about your interviews?" Blake asked. "Did you get all your interviews this week?"

Horton shrugged. "I've got just one left."

"I don't believe you. Let me see your interview book."

"I don't have it."

"What do you mean you don't have it?"

"It's down there on a bench."

"Well, hurry up and go fucking get it!"

The pledge sneer slightly before sluggishly walking down the multilevel staircase. His defiant attitude enraged my roommate.

"I said hurry!" Blake yelled.

Horton continued at the same leisurely pace which sent Blake charging down the stairs after him.

"If I get it first," Blake threatened, "I'm gonna fucking burn it and you'll have to start all over again!"

I laughed and listened to the clanging sound of feet running on metal stairs.

"Run, bitch, run!" Blake screamed.

Both young men were hustling down the staircase at maximum velocity. My roommate probably had a good chance of catching the pudgy kid until he turned his ankle.

"Ow!" Blake yelped. "Ow! Ow! Ow!"

* * * * *

"So you guys haze your pledges a lot?" Kevin asked.

I shrugged. "No more than they deserve."

"You like hazing em?"

Blake smiled venomously. "Yeah. We like it a lot."

The technician laughed and continued to joke with us about hazing and our proclivity for sustaining injuries. We were at the Tallahassee Orthopedic Clinic, sitting in a large rectangular room with two rows of examination tables. X-rays and CAT Scans decorated the walls and numerous patients were being treated for bone injuries.

A fat, middle-aged woman with stringy grey hair sat across from us and she looked very pleased that her arm cast was coming off today.

"Yes, sir," she told the doctor. "I'm just tickled that I can finally run the washing machine again all by myself."

"You need both arms to run it?" asked the doctor.

"No, precious! I need two arms to pour in the water

jugs."

"Ahhh," he said, eyes cast downward at his clipboard. "The water loading mechanism is broken?"

"For heaven's sakes no," she said. "My husband don't trust the city water round here. We buy water jugs at the grocery store and pour em in. Now I can finally do it without him helping me!"

The doctor looked up at his patient and she smiled a teethy smiled that was missing several teeth.

Ten more minutes passed before one of the busy doctors finally treated Blake. Dressed in a white medical coat, he was a thin, weasel-looking man with glasses who periodically spoke into a recording device to chronicle what type of injury he was treating. When he approached Blake, he offered a friendly handshake and casually examined the X-Ray hanging behind us.

"Well," he said, "since I see no sign of a fracture, it looks like we're dealing with a severe sprain."

Blake seemed pleased. "Hell yeah, yo."

"Actually, young man," remarked the doctor, "a sprain is in many ways worse than a break."

My roommate's shoulders slumped. "Hell no, yo."

"I'm going to recommend that you not do any weight-bearing on the ankle for at least two weeks…"

Blake was foolishly playing basketball a few days later.

"…and I'm going to write you a prescription for pain medication and three weeks of physical therapy to strengthen the injured area."

Blake lazily did not do any of the therapy and he shared the pain killers with his boys.

When the doctor left us, Kevin set Blake up in a soft cast and used a wheelchair to roll my roommate out the front door of the hospital. I pulled my car up to the curb and Blake literally hopped in.

"I need some fucking crutches," he grumbled.

"Too bad I left mine in Atlanta."

"How much do they cost?"

"Like twenty bones."

Blake scowled. "Fucking Horton."

I busted a left onto Capital Circle and drove down the road to Eckerd's drug store. When we pulled into the lot, I blew past the front entrance and headed towards the pharmacy drive thru.

"Yo, where you going?" Blake asked.

"Fuck Eckerd's. I'm not walking in there wearing my moon boot to buy you some crutches. They can pass that shit through the window."

Blake laughed and shook his head. "Yo, they're not gonna give us crutches through the pharmacy drive thru."

"Trust me. I've done this shit before."

"With Allison?"

"Yeah. After Desperado. Right before we got into a car wreck."

Blake looked away and mumbled, "My bad, Bryce. I should've been there to stop the car accident instead of hooking up with that girl Erica."

"Fuck that. You *should've* been there to stop me from jumping over the fire!"

My roommate laughed as we pulled up to the drive thru. A young man in a lab coat appeared at the window.

"Can I help you?" he asked.

"Yeah," I replied, "my boy needs some crutches."

Five minutes later, we were cruising down Tennessee Street with a brand new pair of wooden crutches. When we neared campus, I saw a familiar sight fifty yards ahead of us.

"No fucking way!" I exclaimed. "There goes Lugar!"

"Where?"

"Right there!" I pointed towards a lanky kid rolling down the sidewalk on a skateboard.

Blake peered closer and shook his head. "Nah, yo. That

ain't him, but it looks like that fucking asshole."

The skater flew past us and I saw that Blake was right.

"Must be his distant cousin," I said. "I hope he crashes on that thing and does a face plant."

Blake grinned. "I still can't believe we didn't get into more trouble for what we did to that guy."

"I know, right? Remember when we were at Chapter and Mad Dogg came running over to the Upsilon House to tell us Lugar was calling the cops?"

"Yeah, but he told the dorm manager instead and that fat fuck just moved him to a different room." Blake laughed. "That was awesome! I had my own room after that."

I glanced at my friend. "I can't remember…why were you so pissed that night? What'd Mad Dogg tell you Lugar said behind your back?"

Blake shrugged. "It was something about why I shouldn't be blasting rap music all the time, trying to act all ghetto and thuggish because I was adopted and my parents are Jewish."

"Yeah, that was it. You were pissed as fuck."

"I started raging out. Fucking tore down his posters and threw the rest of his shit all over the room."

"You looked like that skinhead Remy from *Higher Learning* when he flips out and trashes his roommate's stuff."

"At least I didn't chuck a loogy on his bed," Blake accused me with a grin.

I shook my head. "That wasn't me. I gleaked on his bed and then John's ass chucks a huge fucking loogy on there that stained his comforter."

My roommate laughed. "Should we feel bad about what we did to that kid?"

"Fuck Lugar. He was anal retentive as hell and he thought he was better than everybody."

"He was stingy as hell too. Remember his secret food stash?"

I nodded. "Remember that time he made a big deal about drinking for free because he didn't get his fair share the night before?"

Blake chuckled. "Hell yeah. He drank like four beers, puked his ass off, and that big girl the Fullback nursed him like a bitch."

"Wasn't that the night you and Mad Dogg took pictures of his toothbrush scrubbing a toilet?"

"Nope!" Blake laughed. "That was a different night!"

We were driving by the Westcott Building now and we stared at the students gathered near the bus stop. Two dark-haired girls were holding Beta sorority bags. They both wore tiny shorts that revealed perfect asses and tan legs. My cock stirred when one of the girls dropped her bag and bent over to retrieve it.

Damn. Maybe I don't want to get back together with Allison.

Blake interrupted my thoughts. "You want to pick up a pizza at Hungry Howie's?"

"You buying?

"Nah," Blake laughed. "Look at us. We look fucking pathetic. They'll give us free pies just because they feel sorry for us."

We did look rather pathetic standing in the pizzeria waiting for our two pies. My roommate was wearing a soft cast and was hunched over on his wooden crutches. I was sporting the huge walking cast that looked like a cyborg leg. A few curious stares were given our way by the other patrons.

Blake shuffled nervously and mumbled, "We look like we just got into a bad car accident."

"Nah, man. We look like a couple of gamblers who didn't pay our bookies and they fucked us up for it!"

My roommate laughed. "Hell yeah, yo. We used to be the Flex Brothers, now we're the Cripple Brothers."

We paid for our pizzas, ate a slice for the road, and returned to the fraternity house to vegetate for a few hours until Quarts on the Court began.

Mitchell called me two hours later. "Yo, what's up juice monkey?"

"You want to lift?" I asked.

"Yeah, you want to hit up the Leach?"

"Nah, let's just do the basement."

"Come on, bro. Let's hit up the Leach Center. I need some eye candy to look at."

"Quarts on the Court will be going on. We can flex for all the little sluts that show up."

"Alright, cool. I'll be there in fifteen minutes."

Mitchell showed up twenty minutes later and we knocked out chest in the basement.

When our workout was done, I exited the basement and observed a crowded courtyard. Rap music was thumping and pickup basketball games were running on the court. Couches had been moved outside and there was a large crowd of brothers, friends, and girls drinking beer and smoking.

"Yo, Bryce!" Blake called from a couch. "Come here!"

"In a minute. I need to get a protein shake."

"Come here first!"

I strolled towards the couches and sat down next to my roommate. His bulldog Salley was lying in front of him.

"What's up?" I asked.

"Thorne and Cortez are going at it."

I shifted my attention to the basketball court. Our Miami brother Cortez was dribbling the ball and our redneck brother Thorne was guarding him.

"Come on, spic boy!" Thorne taunted. "Bring that shit in!"

"Fuck you, gringo!" Cortez hissed.

Thorne pressed his hips into his opponent to prevent him from dribbling closer to the basket. Cortez decided to pass the ball off and then circled around the court. Thorne followed and continued with his taunting.

"Hey, Cortez!" he exclaimed. "Maybe the Cuban national anthem will motivate you. *Row, row, row your boat!*"

Spectators laughed.

Cortez got the ball again and made his move. He pivoted right but then cut back left with a smooth crossover. Thorne was surprised for only a split second, but the fake gave Cortez the advantage he needed and he drove to the basket for the layup. The ball sunk in the basket for two.

"Hey, Thorne!" Cortez yelled as he trotted away. "How do you know you're a dumb fucking redneck? When your dog farts, you claim it!"

Thorne was not pleased. He passed the ball in to his teammate Alex and ran down the court. Cortez was on him like glue.

"Keep running your mouth," Thorne sneered. "Watch what happens if you keep running your spic mouth."

"White trash bitch," Cortez replied. "Nobody's scared of you."

The redneck violently shoved off Cortez with his forearm and was passed the ball. He spun around and nailed a sweet jump shot.

"How'd you like that one?" Thorne taunted. "You fucking saltwater nigger!"

Cortez was pissed. Instead of passing the ball in to his teammate, he flung a hard chest pass at Thorne's head which struck the redneck in the side of his face.

"What the hell?" Thorne grunted in pain.

"Suck my spic dick, bitch!" Cortez snarled.

Thorne charged at Cortez, but the other players grabbed the two young men and restrained them from fighting.

"Fuck you, Cortez!" Thorne screamed. "You fucking beaner!"

Cortez smiled. "How does your face feel bitch?"

Blake and I were watching the quarreling brothers with

much amusement.

"This is hilarious," Blake giggled to me.

"Fucking Thorne," I said. "That guy is always instigating."

"Hell yeah. I hope Cortez punches him in the mouth."

Since the two young men refused to finish the game together, new teams were picked and Thorne decided to sit out and drink beer.

"Watch," Blake said, "I bet Thorne starts talking shit again now that Bill and Clayton are here."

I stared across the courtyard at the bench where Thorne and his redneck buddies were sitting.

"Hey, Cortez!" Thorne shouted. "What does a Cuban do when he gets a flat tire? He drowns!"

The rednecks laughed, but Cortez ignored them and continued to play ball.

I noticed Horton and Patterson were also sitting on the bench with the rednecks, laughing it up like good little peons.

My lip curled. "Look at those fucking pledges sitting over there."

"Yeah, they're definitely a part of the redneck crew now. They've been co-opted."

"Fucking fat ass slobs. They didn't touch the weights once when I was gone, did they?"

Blake shook his head. "I don't think they even lifted when you were here. They would just sign the sign-in sheet and lie about lifting."

"You're probably right. Horton is too soft mentally to handle weights physically."

"And Patterson is just a lazy fuckhead."

"Yeah, he's got Husky Syndrome."

"What the hell is Husky Syndrome?"

"The kid has always been a bigger guy and never had to work for it, but you can't rely on natural strength and size to stick out anymore in a meathead town like Tally."

"Nope," Blake agreed. "You gotta train and you gotta supplement."

"Or juice!" I grunted and flexed my biceps.

"Yo, how's that shit working?"

"Good. It's been two days and I already feel like ass raping every girl I see."

Blake grinned. "Hell yeah. I need to get some of that shit. We should make it mandatory for all the pledges to do a cycle."

I laughed. "Yup. Instead of branding them, we should just shove a needle of testosterone in their asses."

Blake laughed and I continued to watch Horton and Patterson with displeasure. It was far too easy to envision them becoming drunk slobs with a proclivity for fat girls.

"Fuck it," I said. "If they don't want to lift weights, then they can at least pick up the weights *I* lift."

"Good idea."

I stood up and bellowed, "Patterson! Get your butt buddy Horton, bring your donut eating ass down here, and go clean up the weight room!"

The young men grudgingly obeyed their former Pledge Marshall's command and ventured into the basement.

"Dudes were kind of slow to obey," Blake mumbled.

"Yeah, I noticed that. Do you want to go in there and haze them?"

"In the middle of the afternoon?" he laughed.

"Yeah."

"Nah, there's too many girls here. We don't want them to walk in and see us torturing two freshmen."

"Whatever," I said with a shrug. "Hell Week is almost here. There's gonna be plenty of time to haze them then."

Blake chuckled. "I can't wait. Those kids don't even know what's waiting for them."

I sat back down on the couch and watched the basketball game. My hand absently toyed with one of Blake's wooden crutches.

"Fuck hospitals," Blake said, staring at his ankle.

"Hell yeah," I agreed gloomily. "Fuck Eckerd's, fuck pledges, and fuck our ankles."

Blake was quiet for a few seconds before he turned to me and asked, "You think our ankles could be God's way of punishing us for the way we treat pledges and kids like Lugar?"

"You mean what goes around comes around?"

"Yeah, like Karma or something."

I stared at the crutches, I stared at my walking boot, and I stared at Blake's soft cast.

"You know what, kid?" I replied. "It's a possibility I'm not willing to rule out."

CHAPTER SIXTEEN

HELL WEEK II

"Mung these fuckers!"

"Hello?"

"Dude, Mitchell just called me! We've got ten minutes to get to the house!"

"Are you serious?"

"Yeah. Get moving!"

The pledge snapped his phone shut and swallowed. "What is it?" his roommate asked.

"Shit, dude," he said. "We just got called in for Hell Week."

"Fuck! Grab your stuff! Let's go!"

"Wait! We gotta put on jeans and a t-shirt!"

"Damn. I forgot."

"Do you have your condom?"

"Yeah…do you?"

He hesitated. "Yeah…"

"Come on! Let's get this over with!"

The pledge and his roommate changed their clothes, charged out the door, and took the side stairway to the ground. With book bags and duffel bags slung over their shoulders, the two young men humped it across campus like two Marines in boot camp. Strangers who watched them pass by in the night stared in bewilderment. Those more familiar with Greek Life chuckled softly. They knew what was in store for the pledges. Different fraternities had different forms of hazing, but initiation week for a pledge was always Hell Week.

As the pledge ran, he thought about the items he was bringing with him to the Upsilon House. Books, notebooks, and other school supplies. His Pledge Marshall told them that class would be the only reason they could leave the fraternity house. A sports coat, dress pants, and dress shoes. He was required to wear this stuff on campus. A pair of red shorts and a wife beater. This was his house uniform during the day. One FSU card. He knew his big brother would steal this from him to use his flex bucks and meal plan. Ten dollars in quarters was jingling around his front left pocket with every running step he took. Beer money he was told. At least they let him drink during Hell Week. Chewing tobacco, Copenhagen Dip, and Marlboro Lights were in his back pockets along with a pack of Big League Chew. He hoped these weren't for him. The thought of using tobacco made him sick ever since the time he had been forced to smoke an entire carton of Marlboros by the strict priest at his Catholic High School who caught him and his boys smoking in the bathroom. A small red paddle with an Upsilon logo. He prayed this wouldn't be used to spank him in diapers like the movie *Animal House*. And last but not least…one Trojan condom. This was the item he dreaded thinking about the most because he had a pretty good idea what he was supposed to do with this. Rumors had been circulating among his pledge brothers for weeks, but the brothers wouldn't really make him do it, would they? And would any of his pledge brothers actually do it if they were told to? And if they did fuck a bull, *would he?*

The pledge and his roommate sprinted by the SouthGate cafeteria and headed through the passageway to Pensacola Street. A pair of hot sorority girls were smoking cigarettes from a bench.

"Run, Forrest! Run!" yelled one of the girls.

"Suck it, bitch! Suck it!" the pledge screamed in reply.

His roommate laughed and so did he, but they both knew this would be the last sound of laughter either of them would make for days.

The pledge and his roommate hit the sidewalk and

turned up the speed. Two of their pledge brothers were running up ahead of them and he glanced over his shoulder and saw another pledge trailing behind them. The young man was too far back to identify, just a white t-shirt and jeans racing through the night.

The pledge and his roommate were approaching the Upsilon House now, two large white buildings separated by a courtyard. They cut around the side of the house and came to a sudden stop in the back. It was the same spot they met before pledge meetings and Call-Ins. Some of his pledge brothers were already there and the rest of them were on their way. A few brothers were there too, standing on the staircase and the back porches.

Shit! Darren Bryce was there and he was wearing his combat boots, camouflage pants, and black wife beater. He looked bigger than he did a couple weeks ago when he had surprised them with that bullshit "I'm back in town, I want to haze you" Call-In. He looked pissed too. Rumor had it that Bryce had just returned from his grandmother's funeral. Who knew if I guy like that even gave a shit about his grandmother or what kind of mood her death would put him in, but it didn't really matter because everybody knew Bryce was a psychopath who liked to get aggressive for no reason at all.

"Line the fuck up," Bryce growled in his deep voice. "Line the fuck up."

The pledge and his roommate fell in line with the other young men dressed in jeans and white t-shirts.

"Bryce must be roiding," his roommate whispered. "He's starting to look jacked up again."

"SHUT THE FUCK UP!!!" screamed a furious voice. "This is Hell Week! You don't fucking speak unless you're fucking spoken to!"

The spine of the pledge tightened. He recognized the owner of the voice to be Blake, one of the meanest brothers in Upsilon. Blake was definitely a cool guy to hang out with, but during Call-Ins he was a cruel motherfucker who enjoyed making you suffer.

Blake was cursing in his roommate's face now and he had enough tobacco in his mouth to make his lip stick out like a monkey.

"Did you hear what I fucking said?" he snarled. "Don't fucking answer me! Nod your fucking head!"

His roommate nodded his head, eyes cast downward.

Blake was wearing a black wife beater, khaki cargo shorts, and dark brown Lugz boots. His muscular brown arms looked huge tonight and he raised a finger and jabbed it into his roommate's cheek.

"I'll be watching you, motherfucker. You're gonna be my little bitch all week long. I'm gonna take extra special care of you!"

More pledges showed up and fell in line. They were all huffing and puffing from their frantic flight across campus.

"Congratulations," Bryce said bitterly. "You made it on time, but if your entire pledge class doesn't make it here in the next two minutes, then I'm sending all of you home and don't even think about *ever* coming back."

Three more pledges appeared from the darkness and then a few more after them. They showed up in singles, pairs, and triples. Another minute ticked off and a car suddenly blew by the house before coming to a screeching stop. Pledges jumped out and sprinted to get in line.

"That's all of them," Blake announced.

"Alright, pledges," Bryce said as he glared at them hatefully, "come with me."

They reluctantly followed the muscular, shaved-head figure into the gravel parking lot. Cars and trucks filled the lot, many of them with Upsilon stickers on their rear windshields. The pledge planned on getting an Upsilon license plate frame after he made it through Hell Week and earned the right to sport Upsilon letters. *Fucking Horton and Patterson!* He was still pissed at those idiots for wearing Upsilon letters and getting the entire pledge class hazed for it twice.

"Spread out!" Bryce yelled. "Make enough space so you can lie down without lying on top of each other."

The pledge and his pledge brothers spread out nervously, none of them knowing what to expect next, but all of them expecting the worst.

"Now lay down!" Bryce screamed.

The pledge lay on gravel and stared at the feet of his pledge brother in front of them. The soles of the sneakers had been worn down and there was something that looked suspiciously like gum on the heel of his friend's left foot.

It was silent for a few moments until he heard the sound of wicked laughter. Footsteps crunched on gravel as a mob of brothers fell upon them.

"Welcome to Hell Week, bitches!"

"Give me fucking cigarettes!"

"They better of brought Camel Lights!"

"Fucking pledges!"

Rocks were kicked on him and he felt hands reach into his pockets and pull out his tobacco products.

"Thanks for the smokes, pledge," a brother said and gleaked spit on his neck. "Thanks a lot."

"Don't worry, bitch," he heard another brother say to the pledge next to him. "I'm not stealing your condom."

"Moo moo moo, you fucking pledges," said another brother with a snicker.

A few feet away, he saw a brother use his foot to sweep gravel rocks onto two pledges before walking off with a laugh. *Fucking asshole!*

Brothers cleared out and their cruel voices faded away. It went silent again and the pledge stared at shoe soles, straining to hear what would happen next. The first sound he heard was that of a single man walking slowly through the gravel parking lot. It was followed by the stern voice of his

Pledge Marshall.

"Welcome to Hell Week," Mitchell said. "Reach into your front left pocket and pull out all forty quarters."

The pledge reached into his pocket and tried to pull out the change. It wasn't easy to grab all of the quarters, but he got most of them and then went back for the rest.

"Very good," the Pledge Marshall said mockingly. "Now hold them up high so I can dump them in this bag."

The pledge cupped his hands together and held them up like he was making an offering to the gods. It seemed like forever for the Pledge Marshall to finally get around to him. Rocks were stabbing into his chest and his shoulders were growing tired from holding up the quarters. He closed his eyes and gritted his teeth.

"Quit squirming," Mitchell said as he stepped in front of him. "And hold them up higher."

The pledge strained to hold his cupped hands higher. Quarters were plucked from them and he heard the jingling sound of coinage being dropped into a bag.

"Alright," Mitchell said as he moved on to the next pledge. "Hold your fucking hands higher and stop fucking squirming."

When all the quarters were finally collected, the Pledge Marshall slowly walked away. The pledge listened to the sounds of feet crunching gravel and then there was only silence. Seconds ticked off and turned into minutes. The pledge knew the brothers were preparing something for them. He was certain it would be something cruel. *But what?*

"Get your bags and line up!" Bryce's deep voice bellowed from behind them.

The pledges climbed to their feet, turned around, and slung their bags over their shoulders. Bryce was standing in front of them with a beer in his hand.

"It's almost time, gentlemen," he said. "Go to the back staircase. Backstreet is waiting for you."

They marched in a single file line and saw Backstreet standing on the staircase that led up through the rear building of the fraternity house. The muscular, blonde-haired young man was dressed in a black wife beater and camouflage pants. A cigarette hung lazily from his mouth and he glowered at the pledges as they stood before him. The pledge liked Backstreet. He was a cool bartender who pulled girls, but like Blake, he could be a mean ass sonofabitch when he hazed.

"Can you hear them?" Backstreet asked, eyebrows arched in amusement.

The pledge strained his ears, but heard nothing.

"Don't worry," Backstreet said and took a drag from his cigarette. "You will."

Ten more seconds passed before the pledge heard the brothers. They were gathered on the other side of the building in the courtyard and it sounded like hundreds of them. Yelling. Cursing. Laughing. All of them with the same cruel note in their voice. Playground bullies. Torturers. Assholes. The pledge was growing nervous. He wasn't a pussy, but that didn't mean he couldn't dread something he knew he was going to hate.

The pledge suddenly felt a bug biting his neck. He slapped his hand at the insect and it fell down his t-shirt, stinging his chest and stomach. But when he lifted his shirt and the bug fell out, it wasn't a bug. It was a cigarette butt.

Backstreet smiled at him and flicked his tongue ring.
Asshole!

"Listen up, pledges," Backstreet said. "When I give the order, you're gonna run up these stairs and follow me into the basement." He grinned and added, "You're gonna *try* to follow me into the basement."

The pledge tried to guess what this meant, but Backstreet did not give them any time to think about it.

"Let's go, bitches!" he yelled and spun around.

The brother charged up the staircase and the pledges

followed. They ascended the stairs, sprinted through the narrow hallway, past the apartments, and hustled down the staircase into the courtyard where over seventy brothers were lined up in two single file lines leading into the basement. Many of the brothers wore camouflage and some even had ski masks on. They were all screaming and yelling.

"Come on, you fucking pledges!"

"Welcome to Hell Week!"

"Get in the basement!"

"Get the fuck in the basement!"

"Welcome to Hell Week!"

The pledge saw his pledge brothers in front of him being denied passage. They were shoved, slammed into, and struck with fisted body shots. One pledge was knocked to the ground, and when he got up, he was body-checked down to the pavement again. And then another pledge went down. And then another. It was a gauntlet and they were the prey. The pledge watched his friends being pummeled and then it was him fighting off the brothers who cursed, spit, and snarled in his face.

"Fuck you, pledge!"

"Welcome to Hell Week!"

"Welcome to fucking Hell Week!"

"Fuck you!"

He caught an elbow in the eye, a brother's maybe? Or maybe a pledge thrown backwards. It didn't matter. He pressed forward, pushing at the white shirt of his pledge brother in front of him, pumping his legs like he was at High School football practice and his coach was yelling at him to hit the blocking sled like a man.

"Fuck you, pledges!" howled a brother. "Fuck you!"

He was painfully struck in the back with something. A fist probably or maybe even a foot. The blow to his kidney was too precise not to be a deliberate shot. He gritted his teeth and fought them off, using his duffel bag as a shield and a battering ram to follow the white shirt in front of him, knowing that the pledge behind him was probably doing the same.

And then he was there. The dark basement was lit up by a strobe light and he heard the uninviting sounds of *ACDC's* "Hell's Bells" ringing out from the large stereo speakers. More brothers were waiting for them inside and they shoved him and his brothers towards the center of the main chamber, jeering at them like prison guards.

"Get in there, pledge!"

"Get the fuck in there!"

"Move your ass!"

The pledge and his pledge brothers bunched together, the lot of them like lambs to the slaughter. Brothers in camouflage swarmed around them and they were all holding something in their hands. Buckets. But buckets of what? He knew he didn't want to know.

"Line up!" Mitchell yelled. "Line up and face the wall!"

The pledges spread out and turned their backs to the gathering monsoon of brothers who were laughing now, laughing and jeering and cursing and yelling. He felt something hit his back hard enough to leave a bruise. It felt like a baseball, but he saw an apple smash against the wall a few paces down from him.

Were the buckets filled with apples? Were they about to be stoned to death with fruit?

The pledge was secretly glad he was closer to the wall than some of his pledge brothers who were inadvertently acting as human shields, but a hand suddenly smacked down on his head and he felt the shattered remains of an egg being rubbed into his hair. And then another egg was smashed on his head, its shell cracking, its yolk splattering.

Were the buckets filled with eggs too?

"Back up, brothers!" screamed a deep voice that sounded like Bryce. "Back the fuck up and shut the fuck up!"

Brothers quieted down and the pledge heard the ominous sounds of *ACDC* continue to drone from the speakers. Someone was hitting the repeat track button so that the doomful bell-ringing of "Hell's Bells" played over and over again. His instincts told him this was the calm before the storm. His instincts were right.

"Alright, boys!" Mitchell yelled. "Let em have it! Mung these fuckers!"

Liquid gushed over the pledge's shoulder and down his body. He lifted his arms and saw a pinkish-orange sludge on his skin. It smelled terrible. Worse than anything he had ever smelled before. Sour milk, ketchup, rotten eggs, beer, and something else, he couldn't quite place it, and then he knew. Urine. The realization was almost as shocking as feeling an entire bucket of mung being dumped right on his head. He doubled over in misery.

It stinks! Oh my god, it fucking stinks! And it was everywhere. On his face, in his ears, in his hair, even in his mouth. *Oh my god, it was in his fucking mouth!*

He gagged and his stomach convulsed, but he fought the urge to puke as he spit the foul tasting slop off his lips and out of his mouth. More buckets of mung were thrown on him until he had lost count of how many times he was dumped with the foul smelling liquid. Another apple pelted him in the back and he heard the pledge next to him screaming.

"My eyes! They're burning! You fucking assholes! They're burning!"

A brother grabbed the agonizing young man and dragged him away, hopefully to the bathroom to wash out his eyes.

"Shit! Shit! Shit!" screamed another victim. "My fucking eyes!"

The pledge squeezed his own eyes shut and was pelted in the back with something, this time much harder than before. Pain caused him to take a stutter step forward and he nearly slipped. The mung was everywhere now, an entire basement floor covered with the pinkish-orange muck, its stink rising up like the steam of a Jacuzzi.

"Alright, pledges," Mitchell yelled. "I want you fuckers down in this shit right now! Lay the fuck down and make snow angels!"

The pledge sat down and lay back in the mung as quickly as possible. There was no point trying to tiptoe in the shallow end. Weakness would only encourage brothers to haze him more, so he plunged into the filth and started flapping his arms and legs. His pledge brothers were right there with him in the muck, flopping and flapping, feeling the nasty slop flying in all directions.

Brothers laughed and cheered them on.

The pledge gave a good performance, hoping this would spare him from being singled out, but it only caught their attention and he was rewarded with another bucket of mung thrown on his chest that splashed up his neck and onto his face.

"Roll over!" Mitchell screamed. "I want you fuckers to do pushups in this shit!"

The pledge rolled over into the pushup position and his eyes immediately started burning. He couldn't tell if this was from the stench rising from the floor or if mung juices had trickled down his hair into his eyes. It didn't matter. His body, the floor, his pledge brothers—they were all one big shit mess now and he was right there in the middle of it.

"Up!" Mitchell yelled.

The pledge pressed up.

"Down!"

The pledge lowered and screamed, "One!"

"Up! Down!"

"Two!"

"Up! Down!"

"Three!"

Over and over again, the pledge and his pledge brothers did countless pushups in the mung. Pinkish-orange muck was everywhere, even inside his jeans, slithering down his butt crack, in-between his legs, and under his balls. And the smell wasn't get any better. Mung wasn't something you got used to. No, it actually seemed to be getting worse.

And then he knew why. The pledge heard the retching sound of young men vomiting all around him which added more vile stenches to the harsh, vaporizing smell permeating from the sludge.

It smelled terrible! Fucking terrible!

The pledge wanted to vomit again. He tried to fight it, but it came up anyways, out his mouth, and out his nose. He puked and smelled his puke and the smell of his pledge brothers puking and he puked some more.

"Come on!" Mitchell screamed at them. "Keep doing pushups! Up! Down! Up! Down! Up! Down!"

The pledge wanted to quit. He wanted this to be over. His nose was burning. Tears were in his eyes. Nothing was worth this. Nothing.

Fuck the brothers! Fuck Upsilon! Fuck everyone and everything!

And then Blake was suddenly down in the muck, doing pushups with him, his snarling mouth just inches from the pledge's face.

"Come on, kid!" Blake yelled. "Keep going! Up! Down! Up! Down! Up! Down!"

The pledge started doing pushups again and Blake continued to snarl at him like a wild animal.

"Yeah, motherfucker, yeah! Up! Down! Up! Down!"

The pledge repeatedly pushed and lowered his body. He hated Blake for being there and he hated him for cursing in his puking face. Hated him and loved him. If a brother was willing to do pushups in this shit, then so was he.

"Come on!" Blake yelled. "Show me you want to be my brother! Show me you deserve to be here! Get pissed! Show me the Monster! Up! Down! Up! Down!"

The pledged screamed in fury and continued to knockout pushups. He was fired up now. He didn't care about the smell or the taste or the oozing touch of mung on his skin. All he cared about was doing pushups with this crazy motherfucker Blake who he desperately wanted to one day call him brother.

"Up! Down! Up! Down! Up! Down!"

He did more pushups than he had ever done before. More than he knew was humanly possible.

"Up! Down! Up! Down! Up! Down!"

He could do it. He wasn't going to quit. He was going to survive this shit and no one was going to stop him.

"Up! Down! Up! Down! Up! Down!"

Upsilon, Upsilon, Upsilon. He wanted to be a fucking brother!

And then it was over and the pledge and his pledge brothers were taken outside into the cool spring night. They were a sorry sight to look at, drenched in mung, their white shirts forever stained by the pinkish-orange sludge. Pledges with shaved heads had fared better than those with longer hair which soaked up the mung that was now calcifying in lumpy chunks.

"Line up!" Mitchell yelled. "Line up!"

The pledges formed a line and waited.

"Creed Speak!" yelled a brother.

The pledge and his pledge brothers recited the Upsilon Creed as they watched the Pledge Marshall signal to Backstreet.

The blonde-haired meathead stepped forward with a cigarette in his mouth and the hose in his hands. One by one, he sprayed the pledges down with cold water. Some of them cried out in discomfort. Others remained mute, grateful for any form of bathing, regardless of how cold the water was that washed over them.

When it was the pledge's turn, he dipped his head so

that his hair could be cleaned and saw that the water dripping to the ground was filthy with red Mung juices.

"Alright, pledges!" Mitchell yelled. "I want you to go back into the basement and clean that shit up."

Brothers laughed wickedly and the pledges quickly found out why. Cleaning up the Mung was almost as bad as being forced to wear it because there was no adrenaline rush, loud music, or yelling brothers to distract them. The lights were turned on and the pledges stared down at the pinkish-orange sludge that looked like the lava of an erupted puke volcano.

"Take your shirts off!" Mitchell screamed. "You're gonna use them to push the mung out the doors!"

The pledge and his pledge brothers dropped to their knees and used wadded up t-shirts to wipe the floor clean. It took forever to get it done. His knees were killing him and his eyes never stopped watering from the pungent smell that rose up from the mung like a nightmare that would not end. It was horrible. He'd rather of held his face over a gym toilet after a meathead took a huge diarrhea protein dump.

Combat boots strolled up next to him. The pledge looked up and stared at the shaved head, muscular figure of Bryce. He had a beer in his hand and a Mag-Lite in the other.

Great. Now what?

"Word of advice, pledges," Bryce sneered down at him. "You're gonna be making friendly with that floor all week long, so the better job you do cleaning it up, the less you'll have to smell it when you're doing calisthenics."

The pledge nodded in understanding and scrubbed the floor even harder.

Thirty minutes later, the pledge and his pledge brothers were standing together in another line up in the courtyard. It was late now and the temperature had dropped to the fifties. Most of the brothers had gone home, but a few were hanging out near the fire pit on the courtyard. The pledges had been told they were duty-bound to keep the fire burning the entire Hell Week as a symbolic representation of the fire that would always burn within their hearts for Upsilon. Right now the pledge wanted to pull out his dick and extinguish the flames with piss.

The pledge and his grimy pledge brothers were sprayed down with the hose for a second time, but this did little to nothing to remove the calcified chunks of mung from their hair. They were then led into the bathroom by Mitchell.

He smiled cruelly at them and said, "This is where my pledge class slept during Hell Week and this is where you're gonna sleep. Sweet dreams."

The Pledge Marshall shut the door and left them in darkness. No one said a word. At least not right away. They were too scared this was a trick and brothers would come rushing in there to haze them the second they started talking. So no one did. The only sound was that of the occasional water drop from the sink faucet.

As more time passed, the pledge and his pledge brothers started to relax. A few of them put their backs to the wall and slid down to the ground. Others followed their example until they were all sitting and lying, cramped together on the hard floor.

"This is bullshit!" hissed a pledge. "They don't really expect us to sleep in here, do they?"

"Who gives a fuck?" whispered another pledge. "I'd rather be in here doing nothing than out there getting hazed!"

"Hell yeah," someone agreed. "That was fucking brutal."

"What was that shit they threw on us?"

"I think those fuckers put hot sauce or something in my eyes."

"Me too," said another pledge. "I know who did it."

"Who?"

"Jacob. That guy has never liked me."

"It was probably Thorne. I saw that fucking asshole holding two buckets of that stuff."

"That was the worst smell I've ever smelled."

One pledge snickered. "I was puking in that shit and Blake jumped right down in my vomit."

"Blake is fucking crazy," someone said.

"Fuck Blake."

"Nah, man," someone else replied. "I've got more respect for him than any other brother."

"Me too," agreed another pledge. "He showed us there's nothing we have to do he's not willing to go through himself."

The pledge remained silent. He was far too exhausted to waste his sleep time doing anything other than sleeping. He closed his eyes and the whispers of his pledge brothers slowly faded away and then there was only darkness.

* * * * *

"WAKE THE FUCK UP!!! WAKE THE FUCK UP!!! GET OUT!!! GET THE FUCK OUT!!!"

The pledge opened his eyes and saw Darren Bryce yelling at him and his pledge brothers to wake up. His former Pledge Marshall dragged a few sleeping pledges to their feet and flung them out the door.

"WAKE UP, PLEDGES!!! WAKE THE FUCK UP!!! IT'S 4:30 AM!!! IT'S TIME FOR YOUR MORNING CALISTHENICS!!!"

The pledge groaned, squinted his eyes at the light, and exited the bathroom. Plated weights and dumbbells were waiting for them on the basement floor. Hell Week indeed.

CHAPTER SEVENTEEN

BROTHER TRUST NIGHT

"I don't know, man...I don't know."

Mitchell smirked. "That kid should be blackballed just for being a moron."

"Where'd you find him?" Moody asked.

"In his dorm room."

"How'd you catch him?" Dave asked.

"The stupid fuck answered his phone when I called!"

"Dumb shit," I said. "I went home every day when I was a pledge and I never got caught."

Mitchell looked stunned. "What the fuck do you mean you went home every day?"

"I mean instead of going to my classes, I changed clothes in the Diffenbaugh Building bathroom and just walked home to Salley Hall."

Dave laughed. "You brought a disguise with you to Hell Week?"

"Yup. An extra pair of jeans, a long sleeve shirt, a hat, and a pair black sunglasses."

Mitchell was rubbing his goatee in frustration.

I grinned. "It was nice, dude. I showered. I ate a hot meal. I took naps. I got laid."

"Are you fucking kidding me?" Mitchell asked.

"Nope. I also went home and slept when I was supposed to go to work at Bill's Bookstore."

"That's bullshit," he replied angrily. "The only time I slept our entire Hell Week was when Jacob and I fell asleep on the bus."

"Didn't the bus driver kick you off?" Blake asked.

"Yup," Mitchell chuckled. "We rode around campus on

that thing for like three hours until his shift ended. He kicked us off over at the stadium and we had to walk back to the fucking house."

Dave laughed. "I remember that. Gilman and I took you and Jacob to eat at Sub City afterwards."

The lean figure of Klein walked into the living room from the kitchen. He had been posted as our lookout.

"Are they coming?" Moody asked.

"Not yet," Klein replied. "Mendez is leading the first two blindfolded pledges across the courtyard.

Blake snickered. "They have to go to the basement and eat that nasty shit."

"What is that stuff anyways?" I asked.

Dave laughed. "Toothpaste on crackers and yams on sardines."

"It's fucking *gross* is what it is," Mitchell said and his face soured. "The worst part is the glass of water that gets passed around because of all the backwashing."

Dave grinned. "Did any of you guys think the other rooms were real?"

"What?" Moody asked. "That we were really eating bull dick or jumping on glass? Hell no."

"I did," I replied. "They sat me down in front of the toilet before feeding me, like they expected me to puke that shit up. That made it seem real."

Blake nodded. "I really thought I was drinking bull piss. They gave me that warm beer and told me to drink just a little which made me think they were worried about my health or something."

Dave looked at me and grinned. "Kronic told me you were scared to jump barefooted on the glass!"

Mitchell smiled. "The potato chips?"

I chuckled. "Yeah…I didn't want to do it. Kronic had to yell, 'Don't you trust you big brother?' and then I jumped."

My friends laughed and we continued to exchange Hell

Week stories until there was a knock on the back door. Mendez had arrived with the first blindfolded pledge.

"Who's gonna give the speech?" Klein asked.

"Mitchell," I answered. "He's the best at it."

"Hell yeah," Blake said. "Fucking Five-0."

"Bring him in here," Mitchell said as he interlocked his fingers and cracked his knuckles. "I'll do him up good."

The first pledge to be brought inside was Tom and the kid looked horrible. He was dressed in a filthy white t-shirt and wore a ragged pair of blue jeans. The stressful days and nights of Hell Week had caused his fair skin to turn a ghostly pale color which made his short, curly blonde hair look white.

Klein guided the blindfolded young man through the kitchen and led him to the middle of the living room.

"Turn to your right," Klein ordered. "Now stand still and listen."

The pledge obeyed and Mitchell stood up from the couch. When he spoke, he did so with a somber tone of voice drained of all cheerfulness.

"Tom, you've been led from room to room tonight and you've been put through different exercises to teach you to trust your brothers."

Mitchell's voice became louder. "Tom, all that other shit you did tonight was bullshit. What goes on here in this room is very serious and I want you to think extremely hard about the decision you're about to make because it'll be a decision that affects you for the rest of your life."

Mitchell paused, letting his words sink in so that Tom would feel the gravity of the moment. The young pledge shifted uncomfortably and Mitchell continued.

"Tom, tonight you have to make a very important decision. Tonight you have to decide whether or not you're willing to receive the brand of Upsilon."

The pledge's entire body seemed to tense up as Mitchell continued his speech.

"It's about the size of a dime and it's gonna be put on your ass. This brand will be with you the rest of your life and it will represent your commitment to this brotherhood, its traditions, and its ideals…*forever*."

The pledge shifted uncomfortably again and his hands fidgeted with his t-shirt.

"Tom, I want you to think very hard about whether or not you're willing to make this kind of sacrifice."

Ten long seconds passed before Mitchell finally spoke again.

"Tom, are you willing to accept the brand of Upsilon?"

Silence.

"Tom," he repeated, "do you accept the brand of Upsilon?"

The blindfolded pledge lowered his head, did a few nervous shuffle steps, and mumbled, "I don't know, man…I don't know."

Mitchell was annoyed. "Tom, if you want to be a part of this fraternity, then you have to accept the brand."

More shuffle steps. "I don't know…I don't know."

The brothers in the room stared at each other in shock. Most pledges eagerly accepted the brand. A couple pledges always hesitated, but they eventually accepted the brand after a few seconds of debate. Tom's behavior was thus an anomaly.

"I understand your hesitation," Mitchell said in an effort to sound sympathetic, "but brotherhood means a lot more than joining a fraternity for good times and memories. It's about committing yourself to our ideals and carrying them with you long after you leave this place behind."

The pledge did a few more nervous shuffle steps.

"Tom," Mitchell said more forcefully, "We *want* you to become a brother, but you *have* to accept our brand."

"Okay," Tom finally mumbled. "I'll do it."

Dave stood up and led Tom into the kitchen where

Moody and Klein were waiting with the branding instruments.

"Drop your pants," Moody ordered.

Tom pulled down his jeans and revealed a pale white ass. He was shaking like a fresh fish dropping his pants in prison.

"Now hold still," Moody said and lowered the branding instrument so that Tom could feel its radiating heat.

The pledge flinched.

"Hold still!" Klein urged.

Tom took a deep breath and forced himself to relax.

"I'm gonna count to three," Moody said. "Are you ready?"

The terrified pledge nodded his head and swallowed.

"One. Two. Three!"

Tom felt an ice cold sensation touch his ass and he flinched in surprise rather than pain.

"Scream like it hurt," Moody said.

"Ahhh!"

Brothers laughed and Dave exclaimed, "What do you think we are—a black fraternity? We're not gonna brand you!"

The pledge seemed genuinely relieved and was led out the door by Klein.

To simulate the branding process, two cooking pans had been used by the brothers. One was stuck in the freezer and the other had been heated on the stove. Moody held the hot pan near the ass of the pledge so that the young man could feel its intense heat. After the count of three, Moody removed the hot pan and Klein touched the ice cold pan to the pledge's backside.

"What the fuck is wrong with that kid?" I asked my friends. "I've never seen a pledge that scared to get branded."

Klein nodded at Mitchell. "He believed it. Mitchell's speech was convincing."

"Tom is a smart kid," Dave surmised. "He could've thought all the other trust exercises were just a trick to get him into accepting a real brand he was supposed to believe was fake."

Mitchell shook my head. "Nah, bro. This is Big E's fucking fault."

"Why?" Moody groaned. "What'd Big E do now?"

"He got into an argument with some brothers today and then took Tom with him for a thirty minute car ride."

"Thirty minutes?" Dave repeated. "What'd they talk about for thirty minutes?"

"Who knows?" Mitchell said. "Probably all the reasons why Big E hates Upsilon."

"Why'd he take Tom with him instead of some other pledge?"

"Tom is his little brother."

Moody scoffed. "That's just fucking great."

"Fuck Big E," Blake sneered. "I hate that kid."

Mitchell's lip curled. "He definitely makes the list for top five worst brothers."

Blake sneered again. "Yo, the only reason that motherfucker even got a rush bid last year was because he worked at the gym."

"That guy is fucking terrible," I said. "Remember when he broke Moody's windshield?"

"I thought *you* did that," Dave replied.

"Bryce did do that!" Moody said and glared at me.

I smiled. "Yeah, well, Big E motivated me to do it."

"Big E is the worst," Blake said. "He hits on girls like a complete asshole."

"That was true?" Dave asked. "I remember when you guys tried to get him blackballed for that."

"Hell yeah, it was true," I replied. "The guy will talk to a girl for like two minutes and then ask her to go fuck."

Blake shook his head angrily. "Girls still complain to us about that shit. Some dudes can get away with the cocky approach, but a scummy-looking kid with a bald head and big fucking ears can't."

Our conversation was brought to an end when we heard another knock on the door. Mendez had arrived with the next blindfolded pledge.

"I'm giving the speech this time," Moody said.

"Give me that heated pan," Blake said. "I'm gonna burn one of these asses for real."

CHAPTER EIGHTEEN

FIRESIDE CHAT

"Do you really believe in God?"

Big E was still pissed. I could tell that just by looking at him. He entered the courtyard with a scowl on his face and a menacing look in his eyes. He was pissed, he was a prick, and I pitied the pledges about to deal with his bullshit.

Everett, or Big E as we liked to call him, was a tall and lanky kid who tried to camouflage his premature balding by shaving his head which had the adverse effect of bringing attention to his big ears. I watched those big ears as his long strides took him across the courtyard and sat him down next to me on a bench. Three pledges were standing nearby.

"What's up, Bryce?" Big E asked.

"Sup," I replied. "You're up early this morning."

"9 AM Biology. How long these bitches been up?"

"Since 4:30. I woke them up for their morning workout and shower."

"Shower?" he asked in surprise. "You're letting them shower during Hell Week?"

"Yeah, I sprayed them down with the hose."

We both laughed and turned to face the three young men standing before us. The blonde-haired, husky figure of Patterson was using an old broomstick to stir up the flames of the fire pit. Standing to his left was the broad-shouldered Alex. Like his two pledge brothers, Alex was dressed in red gym shorts and a white t-shirt. The face of the stern young man revealed no emotion as he stared into the fire. Taylor stood on crutches just a few feet away. A week before Hell Week started, the young man broke his ankle wrestling Alex in a drunken roommate brawl. Unfortunately for Taylor, the injury had not spared him from any hazing activities. All three pledges looked tired, ragged, and hungry.

"So where's the rest of em?" Big E asked me.

"Walking to class or cleaning the basement."

He glared at the pledges. "I guess you three will have to do."

The lanky young man leaned forward on the bench with a frown on his face. He was upset about his argument yesterday with our brothers and he wanted to take out his frustrations on the pledges by mentally hazing them.

"I heard you're a religious kid," he said to Taylor with a condescending smirk. "Do you really believe in God?"

"Yes, I do," Taylor replied.

"And you believe there's actually a heaven and a hell?"

"Yup."

Big E snorted. "So like, you really believe some guy named Jesus suffered and died for you and rose from the dead to save you?"

Taylor nodded. "I believe it…and I believe he will save you too."

I fought the urge to laugh. Taylor's nice guy face made it impossible to determine whether or not he was being a smartass.

Big E was not pleased with this answer, but he turned his attention to Patterson.

"What about you?" he asked. "Do you believe in God?"

The husky kid shrugged. "I don't know, dude. There's definitely something out there greater than man."

"Why do you think that?" Big E quickly asked. "What evidence is there? Do you really think all the stories in the bible are true?"

Patterson shrugged again, but his eyes lowered to the fire and he offered no further reply.

Encouraged now that he had finally found his opening,

Big E turned to Alex.

"What about you?" he asked snidely. "Have you read the bible?"

"Yeah, I have," Alex replied, making firm eye contact with the brother.

"Do you believe all the stories in the bible are true?"

"No," he answered, "but I believe in the lessons behind the stories."

I smiled. Three days into Hell Week and the exhausted young man was still capable of offering an intellectual reply.

Big E was growing irritated. "Yeah, like what? What lessons do you believe?"

"Relax, Big E," I interjected. "7:45 in the morning on the third day of Hell Week is not the right time for pledges to be answering these kinds of questions."

"Why not, Bryce?"

"It's just too early for that shit."

This increased Big E's aggravation and he stood up from the bench with his book bag in hand.

"You know what, Bryce?" he asked. "*I* believe hazing should be about more than spraying pledges with hoses and making them do pushups. We need to get inside their heads."

"I agree with you, but it's way too early in the morning for that shit."

The reality was I agreed with Big E in principle, but hated seeing losers like him haze alpha males like Taylor and Alex. Watching the tall young man walk off to class, I chuckled to myself in remembrance of the time I tried to get inside *his* head.

"Sit down, Taylor," I said. "Sit down, Alex."

The two muscular pledges sat down in a pair of green plastic chairs while their chubby pledge brother watched them enviously.

"Patterson," I commanded, "go the fuck inside and lift some weights. Maybe another morning workout will burn some flab off your sorry ass."

The pledge dropped the broomstick and slowly walked off with a sulking expression on his face.

"Hey!" I shouted after him. "If I come in there and you're not working-out, I'm gonna put you on the fucking wall again, bitch!"

His pace sped up and he quickly ducked inside the basement doorway.

I chuckled softly and turned my attention to the young men sitting before me. Unlike Patterson, Alex and Taylor were two pledges I wanted to become brothers. My demeanor towards them was thus very different.

"So how you boys holding up?" I asked.

"We're doing okay," Taylor replied.

"I'm sorry you had to deal with Big E's bullshit interrogation. Alex, I warned you about guys like him."

Alex shrugged. "We've dealt with it this far, we can deal with it a little longer."

"It's a mental game with guys like that," Taylor said.

"Yeah, it is," I replied and a tiny smile curled on the corner of my lips. "Did you know we tried to blackball Big E when *he* was a pledge?"

"Really?" Taylor asked.

"Yeah. He earned himself a bad reputation because of the aggressive way he was hitting on women. Since a lot of these girls were bigger girls, that's actually how he got his nickname Big E."

The pledges laughed.

"You guys probably thought it was because he's a tall kid, huh?"

"Yeah," Taylor answered.

"Nope. It's because he's got a BBW fetish."

"BBW?"

"Big beautiful women."

The pledges grinned.

"Anyway, we couldn't get him blackballed, so a few of us decided we'd force his ass to quit during Hell Week."

If the two exhausted young men had been half asleep, I definitely had their full attention now. They both sat forward and listened attentively to my story.

"One night we were in a car, hazing his ass pretty bad. He was in the backseat with Backstreet, Blake was driving, and I was riding shotgun. We were all drunk, we had heavy metal blasting, and I got so fired up that I punched out the windshield."

The eyes of the pledges widened.

I chuckled. "Yeah, and the car was Moody's. He was going through Hell Week too, and since I didn't have wheels freshman year, I stole his keys and joyrided that hooptie all week long."

"Was Moody pissed about his windshield?" Alex asked.

"No...not really, but I had to drop like a hundred bucks to fix it and Big E's bitch ass didn't even quit."

Both pledges laughed and Alex said, "I would've paid money to see Big E's face when you broke that windshield."

I stood to my feet and picked up the stick Patterson had been using to tend the fire. The flames crackled as I stirred things around and a few ashes danced in the light morning breeze. Throwing the stick to the ground, I sat back down and resumed our fireside chat.

"So did either of you see Big E storm out of here yesterday?"

"We heard about it," Alex answered.

"Did Tom tell you what Big E said to him during their car ride?"

"No," Taylor answered. "He didn't tell us anything."

Alex used both of his hands to rub the back of his shaved head. He looked tired and angry, but the brooding young man almost always looked angry.

"Tom didn't say shit," he said "That guy never says

shit. He's been reclusive as hell ever since his boy Luke quit. I don't even know if he really wants to be a part of this place."

"What about you two?" I asked, leaning back against the bench. "Do you still want to be brothers of Upsilon?"

"Yeah," Taylor immediately replied.

Alex was slower to answer. "Yeah…but I've got to admit, I've had my doubts."

"We've *both* had doubts," Taylor agreed. "But we're definitely on board now that you're back."

It sucked that Alex and Taylor were not completely confident in their decision to join Upsilon, but that was exactly why I wanted these two young men to be my brothers—they were hungry for more than Upsilon was providing and they had the capacity to achieve more.

"Gentlemen," I said, "I have my doubts every day. There's a lot of guys in this place that I don't like and I don't respect. But there's also a lot of guys in here that I do respect and some that I really do consider to be brothers."

"We see that, Bryce," Alex said. "You and your boys; Rowdy and his crew; Cortez and those guys; Fick, McMillan, and that whole group. All you guys act the way a real brotherhood should."

I nodded. "Never doubt that there's some true motherfuckers in Upsilon—guys who'll throw down for you, guys who'll stick their neck out for you, guys you can trust to sleep in the same bed with your drunk girlfriend."

"There's definitely some solid guys here," Taylor said.

"There is," I agreed. "And gentlemen, things *are* getting better—and they're only going to get better. The right guys are finally starting to take control and steer us in the direction we need to be going."

"We see that too," Taylor said. "The younger guys are wielding more power and cooler brothers are starting to represent us on campus."

I nodded. "That's one of the big reasons I want you

guys for brothers, because I know you know what needs to be done. You guys are the future leaders of this place."

Both young men beamed by my words.

"Taylor," I said, "you're the president of your pledge class for a reason. Your pledge brothers respect you as a person and a leader and so do the brothers. You'll be president of this place one day."

I glanced away from Taylor to face his roommate.

"And Alex...you've got Pledge Marshall written all over you. You're just the kind of guy we'll need to put some backbone into our pledges."

Alex smiled, intrigued by the thought of scaring the shit out of future generations of pledges.

"I'll tell you boys something else too. Other fraternities might not have guys like Big E, but most of them are cloning machines. They suck in decent guys who become fake people without any real substance. They all look, talk, and act exactly the same."

Alex's lip curled. "They're fucking replicas."

I nodded. "When I was bouncing, I had to deal with those kids every Saturday night at the club."

My voice became an impersonation of a typical FSU fratboy, which was a strange blend of preppy-surfer-thug.

"Bro, let's do another shot, we're gonna get sooo gross tonight! Dude, look at our clothes and our hair, we look so fucking good right now we could pull any girl we want. We're tough, dogg. We're on juice. And if anyone fucks with us, we'll get twenty guys to fight him!"

The pledges laughed and my voice reverted back to normal.

"Clones, man. Pussified fucking clones. But that shit doesn't happen here, at least not like other places. Yeah, I want you to hit the gym and maybe even wear a nice shirt when you go out, but it's not about changing who you are so you can be like everyone else—it's about making you maximize who you already are."

The young men nodded in complete agreement.

"Gentlemen," I said, "I just hate seeing guys waste their potential. *That's* why we've been riding Horton and Patterson so damn hard. The last thing Upsilon needs is two more lazy slobs who hang out at redneck bars and hook up with Meat Locker quality women."

Taylor toyed with one of his crutches. "We definitely agree with all that, Bryce. We agree with just about everything you and Mitchell have ever told us. But you guys *have* been riding Horton and Patterson pretty hard."

"Should we not be?" I asked. "Do you really want those kids to be your brothers for the next three years?"

The affable young man shrugged. "I don't really have a problem with them...but Patterson *is* a near talker who has no idea what personal space means. Anytime I talk to him, I can tell you exactly what he ate that day from his breath."

I laughed. "What about Horton?"

Taylor scratched his head. "Man, I don't know. I guess Horton whines a lot."

Alex snorted. "A lot? All that kid ever does is whine. He whined his way back in here after he dropped out a month ago and he's been whining his ass off every second of Hell Week."

Taylor reluctantly agreed. "Yeah, you're right. But he *does* have a shoulder injury."

"And how does that make *you* feel," I asked Taylor who was holding a pair of crutches. "He starts crying about his shoulder and you haven't even complained once!"

"Yeah...I guess it's kind of a bitch move."

Alex smirked. "I don't even think Horton's shoulder injury is legit. He just doesn't want to have to do pushups with the rest of us."

Taylor grinned. "He probably bought that fucking sling he's been wearing from Walgreens."

"Pledges," I said in a solemn voice, attempting to

imitate Big E's earlier performance. "Do you believe the stories of Horton are real? *Do you?*"

The young men laughed.

"Yeah, the timing of his injury is just a little *too* convenient. We're not buying it either. That's why he's been singled out."

Alex spit to his left, away from the fire. When he turned back to face me, his head shook with contempt.

"You know what really bothers me?" he asked. "The holier-than-thou attitude those two have from hanging out with the redneck older brothers, especially Horton. They walk around here like they're the shit, like they're already brothers."

Taylor nodded. "That *is* annoying."

"It's disrespectful as fuck," I said. "The younger brothers are fed up with that shit and want to get rid of them for good. What do you two think about that?"

Taylor shrugged. "We trust brothers like you, Blake, and Mitchell will do the right thing. You guys know better than anyone what needs to be done."

"That trust means a lot," I replied. "Pretty soon you two are gonna be the younger brothers. When I was in your position, I had zero faith in what the older brothers were doing."

Standing up off the bench, I stirred up the fire again with the broomstick and then started walking towards the basement.

"I'm gonna check on Patterson," I said. "If you hear a loud scream, that'll be the sound he makes when I drop a dumbbell on his chest."

The pledges laughed.

Before entering the basement, I turned back around and said, "We couldn't get Big E to quit, but I promise you that won't be a mistake we repeat with Horton and Patterson."

CHAPTER NINETEEN

THE RACK

"Don't fucking drop!"

"Hold him still, goddamnit!" yelled a brother.

"Shut that motherfucker up!" screamed another brother.

The bull snorted and grunted, his mighty hooves stomping on a metal surface. The large animal was not happy and he refused to calm down. He mooed in agitation and grunted and stomped some more.

"Settle him down!" screamed a brother. "Settle him the fuck down!"

"Get that big fucker ready!" yelled another brother.

The Pledge Marshall's voice rose ominously above that of the shouting brothers. Like the other Executive Officers, Mitchell was dress in a red and white robe.

"Alright, you fucking pledges," he said, "are you ready to become brothers of Upsilon? Pull out your condoms and drop your pants! It's time to fuck a bull!"

None of the blindfolded pledges heeded Mitchell's command. Dressed in blue jeans and t-shirts, they stood motionless in the light of the bonfire with their hands clasped behind their backs.

Brothers stomped on the flatbed of a truck and the stereo continued to play the loud sounds of a bull grunting and mooing. To blindfolded pledges, it should have sounded like a real bull. It did when I was a pledge.

"I said drop your pants!" Mitchell yelled. "Start jerking your little dicks and get them hard!"

None of the pledges moved.

"What the fuck is wrong with you?" he screamed

furiously. "Drop your pants right fucking now!"

Blake and I stood a few yards away with a pack of brothers clad in camouflage. The behavior of the pledges was shocking to us all. Some pledges always refused to drop their pants, but other always did. That none of them did tonight indicated our worst fears were true.

"Damn," I whispered to Blake. "They know…they fucking know."

"Fucking redneck brothers," Blake hissed. "What the hell did they think was gonna happen?"

Moody was equally incensed. "Are you fucking kidding me? These little shits have been told everything!"

"What the fuck do we do now?" I asked.

"Fuck these kids!" Blake snarled and charged towards the pledges. When he was within range, he began to furiously kick dirt on them as he repeatedly screamed, "Fuck you! Fuck you! Fuck you! Fuck you!"

I joined him and so did many other brothers. We looked like an army of pissed off baseball coaches kicking dirt on umpires. Our legs dropped back and we swept the dirt up onto the pledges who began coughing and sneezing from the dust cloud rising into their noses and mouths.

Mitchell and the rest of the Executive Officers tried to sustain order, but it was no use. The young men in their red and white robes were no match for the enraged pack of brothers in camouflage who continued to kick dirt on the pledges and curse at them with fury.

"Bryce!" Mitchell exclaimed and grabbed me by my shoulders. "What the fuck is going on?"

"The know everything!" I snarled. "The rednecks told Horton and Patterson about everything to expect during Hell Week and those two little shits told their entire pledge class!"

"So they know the bull is fake?"

"They know everything!" I repeated.

Mitchell's face tightened and his hazel eyes looked

murderous.

"Fuck this shit," he said through gritted teeth. "Get the pledges in the cars and back to the house. We're gonna haze them all night long and I'm gonna make them have an extra day of Hell Week."

His words pleased me. I whirled around and seized Blake and Backstreet by the arms.

"Come on!" I yelled. "Get Horton in your car. Mitchell wants us to haze these kids all night long back at the house!"

The wolf pack duo of Backstreet and Blake snatched the blindfolded pledge and dragged him off into the night. Out of the corner of my eye, I saw other pledges being shoved and pulled away from the bonfire. Rowdy and Jacob had the husky Patterson in their clutches.

Good. They'll give him what he fucking deserves.

Blake ripped open the back door of his car and Backstreet flung the chubby pledge into the backseat. The kid landed on his shoulder sling arm and didn't even flinch.

Fucking Faker!

We all climbed into the vehicle and Blake peeled out of the dirt road parking lot with the diabolical sounds of *Rob Zombie* blasting from his speakers. The wolf pack and I immediately started hazing Horton with unadulterated cruelty.

"CREED SPEAK!!!"

"YOU'RE NOT GONNA BE A BROTHER!!!"

"YOU'RE A FUCKING BITCH!!!"

"WE DON'T WANT YOU!!!"

"YOU FAT PIECE OF SHIT!!!"

"YOU FUCKING LOSER!!!"

"TAKE THAT SHOULDER SLING OFF!"

"WE KNOW YOU'RE FAKING!!!"

"YOU CRYBABY BITCH!!!"

"ALPHABET SPEAK!!!"

"I FUCKING HATE YOU!!!"

"WE DON'T FUCKING WANT YOU!!!"

"CREED SPEAK!!!"

Rowdy and Jacob were no doubt administering a similar treatment to Patterson in their car, and when we arrived back at the fraternity house, the two pledges were both in a meltdown.

"Come on guys," Horton pleaded to some of his pledge brothers in the courtyard. "Let's just quit. This isn't worth it."

"Yeah, guys," Patterson whined, "I'm not putting up with this crap anymore."

The pledges ignored them and were led off by brothers to be hazed.

"Fuck them," Horton sneered to Patterson. "Let's get our shit and go!"

The duo walked into the basement, went straight into the weight room, and started packing their bags. My friends and I gathered at the doorway.

"Good!" I yelled. "Pack your shit up and quit like the bitches you are!"

"Fucking faggots!" Jacob snarled. "Hurry the fuck up!"

"Get your shit out of my house!" Backstreet screamed.

"You fat fucking bitches!" Blake yelled. "Go fucking home and don't ever come back!"

More younger brothers jeered at the young men as they walked by us with tearful eyes and ashen faces.

"You fucking pussies!"

"We don't fucking want you!"

"Get the fuck out of here!"

The duo exited the basement and crossed the courtyard towards the side exit. Blake and I moved to the doorway to watch.

"This is it!" he exclaimed gleefully. "They're gonna fucking quit!"

"Nope," I replied. "Look at *this* bullshit."

Horton and Patterson were intercepted by a pair of

redneck older brothers. They hurriedly guided the emotionally battered duo towards the wooden deck stairway that lead up to Jake's apartment.

"Yo, fuck this shit!" Blake said with a bitter sneer. "I'll fucking kill *all* of them!"

He started out the door, but Rowdy and I restrained him from charging. The enraged young man struggled furiously against us.

"This shit ain't over!" he yelled at the two pledges and the brothers gathering in their defense. "Protect your little babies now, but this shit ain't over until they quit!"

"Don't worry," I said. "They're gonna quit. They won't survive the rest of Hell Week."

"They're fucking done," Rowdy agreed. "We'll fucking break them."

Blake ceased his struggling. "Fuck those kids! I'm gonna put the rest of them on the Rack right fucking now."

Rowdy and I watched the angry young man stomp off towards the weight room.

"Taylor! Alex!" Blake yelled. "Get your asses in here and bring your fucking pledge brothers!"

"What the hell is the Rack?" Rowdy asked me.

I chuckled. "Some hazing technique Blake learned on his pledge road trip to the University of Alabama."

"They got hazed on their road trip?"

"Yeah. Real bad. Especially Blake because of his skin color. The Alabama brothers made him hang from the ceiling rafters over and over again."

"Who were the brother chaperones?"

"Corbin and Preston. Supposedly they just stood around laughing."

Rowdy snorted. "No wonder Blake tried to fight Corbin last semester."

"Come watch," I said and started walking towards the weight room. "Blake might hate Alabama brothers, but he loves teaching our pledges the Alabama way of hazing."

When I entered the weight room, Taylor was hanging from the pull up bar as his pledge brothers anxiously waited for their turn on the Rack.

"Hang!" Blake screamed. "Hang, motherfucker, hang! Show me your dedication to Upsilon! Show me why I should let you join my fraternity!"

The young man clung even tighter, his fingers and knuckles turning white from the strain.

"Keep fucking hanging!" Blake yelled. "Don't be a fucking bitch!"

Taylor held for sixty more seconds before his hands finally gave way and he dropped to the ground on his good leg. Blake grabbed Taylor by the rib cage to steady him.

"Good!" Blake screamed in his face. "Good! That's the dedication I want to see!"

Taylor smiled and I handed him his crutches.

"Your turn, Sammy," Blake said. "Get the fuck up there and show me that you deserve to be here!"

The sturdy young man stepped forward and positioned himself under the Rack. A baseball player with a talent for competitive sports, Sammy already knew what it meant to mentally push himself beyond his natural physical capacity. He jumped for the bar and hung.

"Creed Speak!" Blake immediately yelled.

All of the pledges began reciting the Upsilon Creed, including the young man hanging from the pull up bar.

"Alphabet Speak!"

Again the pledges spoke out in unison.

When they finished reciting the Greek Alphabet, I stepped closer to look at Sammy. The mental struggle was in his eyes, the determined brown eyes of a young man who was not going to quit.

"Don't fucking drop!" I screamed at him. "Don't fucking drop! Show us what you got! Show us you deserve to be here!"

The pledge continued to hang as sweat trickled down his face. Seconds counted off and eventually became minutes. When he finally let go of the bar, everyone was impressed by his stellar performance.

Alex was next. The hazing activities earlier in the night had already put the young man in a foul mood. He was a naturally angry kid and being hazed was like throwing gasoline on a fire. Homicidal eyes stared straightforward at the wall as he reached up for the bar and hung.

"Creed Speak!" Blake shouted.

The pledges recited the creed like druids.

"Alphabet Speak!" he yelled.

As they shouted out the Greek alphabet, Blake moved closer to Alex and shoved the hanging pledge whose body rocked from the sudden jolt.

"Don't be a little bitch," Blake jeered at him. "Think about all the brothers who hazed you tonight and what you want to do to them! Think about what you'd fucking do to them right now if you were alone with them in a dark alley!"

Alex screamed with rage as he tightened his grip on the bar and steadied his rocking body. The other young men fed off his anger and started yelling at their pledge brother.

"Come on, Alex!"

"Get pissed, Alex!"

"Come on, motherfucker!"

"Show us the Monster!"

Alex howled even louder.

"Yeah, Alex! Yeah!"

Blake stepped back now, a perverse look in his dark eyes. Many times had I witnessed my roommate haze pledges, but the look on his face tonight was far more sadistic than I had ever seen before. Maybe hazing these pledges on the Rack was Blake's way of exorcising his bad memories from Alabama. Or maybe the madness in his eyes burned so strongly because he finally had the pledges exactly where he wanted them—fired up, and firing each other up.

"Hell yeah," Blake mumbled to himself. "Hell yeah."

My own emotions began to surge and I stepped forward to shove Alex as he hung from the bar.

"Come on, bitch!" I yelled. "I know you got more than that! Get pissed, motherfucker. Get pissed!"

Alex continued to hang, growling and screaming like a caged animal. Of all the pledges, he probably held on the longest. When the shaved head kid did finally let go of the pull up bar, he immediately reached for it again, but instead of hanging, the psycho furiously tried to rip the bar down.

"That's enough, Alex!" I yelled, laughing. "That's enough, man."

He released the bar, but his muscular body continued to shake with rage. Alex was definitely a crazy ass sonofabitch. I smiled proudly at him and pointed to the other side of the weight room.

"Go walk it off, kid," I said.

It was now Tom's turn to face the Rack and the muscular young man should have excelled at this physical form of hazing. But like Brother Trust Night, the dedication Tom showed for Upsilon was less than impressive and he let go of the bar after a pitiful display.

"What the fuck was that?" Blake screamed, more surprised than angry. "That's all you got?"

The pale-colored pledge lowered his eyes in shame, shook his curly blonde head, and did a few shuffle steps.

"I can't do it," he mumbled. "I can't do it."

We stared in disbelief. He looked like a discouraged kindergartner who had given up trying to learn how to ride a bicycle without training wheels.

"Fuck that!" Blake screamed. "You *can* do it! Get up there and try again!"

His pledge brothers were still caught up in the

adrenaline surge and they too screamed at Tom who was repeatedly forced to hang from the bar. But each time the pledge refused to push himself beyond physical exhaustion.

"Damn," Blake whispered to me, "this kid's heart ain't into it."

"Big E fucked his head up," I mumbled.

"Maybe Big E forgot to feed his little brother today and the kid's got shit for energy."

I shrugged and whispered, "Or maybe he's just a high quality pledge who finally realized Upsilon is not the right place for him."

Blake reluctantly nodded. "Yeah…we should probably back off."

"For now," I said evenly. "When they're done with the Rack, we're making them lift weights until they can't lift their arms."

Blake grinned devilishly. "This is fun as shit. I could haze these fuckers all night long."

The Pledge Marshall eventually called an end to the night's activities so the pledges could get a few hours sleep. When he led the young men out of the weight room, their adrenaline had long since vanished. They looked like walking zombies.

Mitchell put them all in the bathroom and came to find Blake and me in the courtyard.

"Those kids are drained," he said with satisfaction.

"What's up with Horton and Patterson?" I asked. "Are they quitting?"

Mitchell rubbed his goatee and said, "You guys almost had them gone. They were both up there in Jake's room, balling their eyes out like bitches. All the older brothers are pissed."

"Fuck the older brothers," Blake cursed.

"Yeah, they tried to get me to come down here and tell you guys to back off."

"What'd you say to that?" I asked.

Mitchell smirked. "I told them if they don't want their little butt-buddies to be hazed, then they shouldn't give them letters to wear on campus and they shouldn't tell those kids everything to expect during Hell Week."

Blake's dark eyes flashed ravenously. "Are they gonna bring Horton and Patterson back out here?"

Mitchell shook his head. "Not right now. They didn't want to bring them back out at all, but I told them to wait until everybody leaves. When you guys are out of sight, they're gonna put those bitches in the bathroom to sleep with the rest of the pledges."

"You sure they'll follow through with that?" I asked skeptically.

"Yeah, Jake wants them to sleep in there too," Mitchell said with a chuckle. "I guess he remembers what it was like for thirty-one of us to be crammed in there."

"Good," I said. "I'll start things up again with them in a few hours. Horton and Patterson are fucking history."

CHAPTER TWENTY

THE CRUELTY OF MEN II

"You missed a spot."

"Wake the fuck up!" I yelled into the bathroom. "Wake the fuck up right fucking now!"

Sleepy-eyed pledges groaned and climbed to their feet.

"It's 4:30, gentlemen! You know what that means. Get out there and grab a weight!"

The pledges sluggishly walked out into the basement for their good morning workout session. I was pleased to see the two missing pledges were back.

"Ready for the next round?" I asked them.

Horton and Patterson glared at me and I smiled. They both looked tired, worn-down, and ready to break.

"Let's start this right!" I yelled at the pledges. "Wall sits with weights straight out in front of you!"

Pledges put their backs to the wall, sat on air, and held their weights out in front of their chests.

"Alphabet Speak!" I screamed.

They recited the Greek Alphabet and then sweated their way through thirty minutes of intense calisthenics. Afterwards, I led the pledges outside and lined them up in the center of the courtyard.

"Stand here," I instructed. "Creed Speak."

As the pledges chanted the Upsilon Creed, I turned on the water faucet and retrieved the hose. They knew what was coming. I had done this every other morning, but foreknowledge and experience spared them none of the discomfort of being sprayed down. And this time, instead of letting the wet pledges dry off and change their clothes, I left them outside in the 50 degree weather.

"It's gonna be a long day," I said to the pledges as I walked off. "A long fucking day."

Blake was watching television when I entered our apartment.

"What're you doing up?" I asked.

"I can't sleep," he complained. "My stomach hurts."

"Did you swallow some dip again?"

"Nah."

"Did you swallow too much cum again?"

He chuckled. "Nah, I think I got the beer shits or something. What're you doing?"

"I just made the pledges do their morning workout and washed them down with the hose."

"Horton and Patterson are back?"

"Yup. I sprayed the fuck out of Horton's fake ass shoulder sling."

"Good," he laughed. "Did you let them change clothes?"

"Nope. They're all huddled around the fire, trying not to catch the pneumonia. Horton and Patterson are probably crying again."

"Do you think they're gonna quit?"

"They want to. I can see it their eyes. I don't know why they haven't done it yet."

Blake shrugged. "Stubbornness. They don't want the last three months of pledging to be a complete waste of time."

"Yeah…well, whatever it is, I'm spreading the word today to haze the shit out of them."

"Hell yeah. Fuck those kids."

A few hours later, a handful of brothers hazed Horton and Patterson in the basement and then ordered the duo to mop up the floor which was covered with mud and beer from the previous night's events. Having endured through five tortuous days of hazing, the pledges had finally reached their threshold and refused to do any more bitch work. Horton even flung his mop stick to the ground.

"Fuck this!" he exclaimed. "I'm sick of you fucking with us and treating us like slaves."

"Me too," Patterson agreed. "You guys have been picking on us all fucking week and I'm done with it. Mop your own damn floor."

"I shouldn't even be doing this," Horton whined. "I'm wearing a goddamn shoulder sling!"

Rowdy and Jacob happened to be puffing cigarettes in the courtyard when a brother came rushing out of the basement to report what was happening.

"Dude!" he exclaimed. "Horton and Patterson are having a meltdown in there!"

"What're they doing?" Jacob asked.

"They just threw their mops down and started cussing at brothers."

Rowdy's blue eyes widened and Jacob's lip curled sinisterly.

"Let's go!" Jacob snarled and flicked away his cigarette.

Rowdy followed his roommate into the basement where the two pledges were still arguing with brothers.

"What the fuck is wrong with you?" Jacob screamed at the pledges. "Do you think you're fucking special?"

"Fuck you, pledges!" Rowdy yelled. "Do you think you're doing anything *we* didn't have to do?"

"I can't mop," Horton replied. "It hurts my shoulder."

The tall figure of Jacob picked up the mop and shoved it sideways into Horton's soft gut.

"Fuck your shoulder!" the brother yelled. "Use your good arm and mop the floor right fucking now or we're gonna turn you over and clean the floor with your hair!"

The floppy-haired Horton was taken aback by this threat, but still did he hesitate.

Rowdy pounced, barking in his face like a drill sergeant with saliva flying off his lips.

"MOP THE FUCKING FLOOR, BITCH!!! MOP THE FUCKING FLOOR!!! MOP THE FUCKING FLOOR!!!"

Horton fearfully turned away from the snarling brother and began to clean the floor. Patterson wisely followed his sidekick's example and the duo laboriously went to work.

Blake and I entered the basement just as the pledges were finishing up. It looked like the pledges had done a really good job because the white basement floor shined like a Mr. Clean commercial. But Jacob was still not satisfied. He stood in the middle of the basement and beckoned to the pledges.

"Leave the bucket and bring your mops over here. Come on! Both of you!"

The two young men dragged their mops to where the tall, red-haired brother was standing. They looked miserable and their shoulders slumped with exhaustion.

"You missed a spot," Jacob said and pointed down at the floor.

I looked and saw a floor that looked perfectly clean.

"Where?" Patterson asked.

"Yeah," Horton sneered. "Where?"

"You don't see it right fucking here?" Jacob asked, pointing at the same spot.

Both young men bent over to take a closer look. Blake and I also strained harder to see. From where we stood, there was absolutely nothing to clean where Jacob was pointing. Patterson must have thought the same thing because he started shaking his head in confusion.

"Where, man?" he asked. "I don't see anything."

Jacob suddenly back pedaled away from the two pledges and Rowdy dumped the large bucket of dirty mop water over their heads.

"Right here!" Rowdy screamed.

The pledges bolted upright, drenched and stunned stupid by the filthy water. Patterson's lips made a motor boat sound as he tried to spit the mop water off them and away from his mouth. Floppy-haired Horton looked like a drenched dog. He howled in pain and wiped at his eyes.

"You stupid pledges!" Jacob laughed.

"Mop that shit up again!" Rowdy yelled.

The two brothers danced away, laughing their asses off like schoolyard bullies. It was a cruel fucking thing to do. *Hell Week indeed.*

"Holy shit," I whispered to my roommate. "Holy fucking shit."

"Damn, yo," Blake said in shock, "those guys are even meaner than we are."

They were apparently mean enough.

"Fuck you, man!" Horton screamed with tears in his eyes. "Fuck you, man! I quit this fucking place!"

"Fuck you guys!" Patterson yelled. "We're done! We're so fucking done with this shitty ass fraternity!"

The duo stalked into the weight room, grabbed their bags, and swiftly exited the basement. This time they did not retreat to Jake's apartment, this time they walked out the courtyard and did not look back.

"Come on," I said to Blake. "Let's go watch them."

Blake and I ran upstairs to our apartment and observed the two freshmen from our window as they walked down the Pensacola Street sidewalk. Both young men were laughing and encouraging one another that quitting was the right thing to do. Horton even ripped his shoulder sling off and threw it to the ground.

"What a fucking bitch!" I said, shaking my head.

"I knew it!" Blake exclaimed with satisfaction. "I knew that motherfucker was lying!"

"I was almost starting to feel bad about hazing him so much."

"Fuck that kid," Blake said with contempt. "I don't feel sorry for anybody."

Meanwhile, Clayton and a few of the redneck brothers had found out about the maltreatment of their two favorite pledges and a heated argument ensued in the basement.

"You guys were out of line pulling that stunt," Clayton angrily told the two younger brothers.

"You need to go after them and apologize," said another older brother.

"That was fucked up," agreed a redneck brother. "I've been here four years and I've never seen pledges treated like that before."

"Good," Jacob replied smugly. "Maybe if some of the losers in our fraternity had been hazed that way, they would've quit."

The noble Bishop chimed in. "I know you don't like those kids and you want them to drop, but what happens if they report you guys? What if we get our charter pulled?"

Rowdy snorted. "That won't happen because they'd also be punishing all you dumb-ass older brothers who thought it'd be a good idea to tell them what to expect during Hell Week."

Clayton shook his head. "You younger brothers have no fucking respect for tradition."

"No," Jacob replied, "we've got no respect for people who won't do what it takes to make this place better."

"This is bullshit," snarled an older brother. "You guys have been brothers for less than two years and you think you've got the right to tell *us* how to run things."

Rowdy laughed. "Fuck off and graduate. We're sick of you old fuckers hanging around."

Tensions elevated and it seemed like violence might erupt until Mitchell intervened.

"Hey! Hey!" he screamed. "It's done with! Horton and Patterson are gone and they're not coming back. You guys need to calm the fuck down or go the fuck home. We got pledges outside right now wondering if they really want to join a fraternity with this much bickering going on."

Mitchell's words had the desired effect. The pissed off older brothers ventured outside and Jacob and Rowdy came up to my apartment.

"Hell yeah!" Blake exclaimed as they entered our living room. "That was fucking awesome!"

Rowdy chuckled. "Screw those kids."

"We just saw Horton rip off his shoulder sling and throw it on the ground."

Jacob smirked. "I *knew* that bitch was faking."

"Let me shake your hands," I said with a smile. "That was some of the best hazing I've ever seen."

Rowdy grinned like a shark. "It's like you always say, Bryce. Real brotherhood means putting the interests of the brotherhood first. We're better off without them."

"For the good of the fraternity," I said and shook his hand.

"For the good of the fraternity," Rowdy repeated.

FRATIRE the series is now available. Please visit www.collegelifeXtreme.com for more information.

TALLAHASSEE

A Sociological Analysis

Florida State University wasn't Harvard, Princeton, or even the University of Pennsylvania. In comparison to these more prestigious universities, I may have lost out academically in my collegiate experience, but what I learned socially from living in a college town like Tallahassee, I doubt very few universities could have matched. If there was ever a place to study human nature, social psychology, and moral behavior, then that place was Tallahassee. Warm sunny weather, tens of thousands of young people, and a fast-paced, competitive social scene heavily influenced by the materialistic culture of South Florida made FSU the ideal laboratory to live the great experiment that is the college experience.

Tallahassee was truly a college town. In a city whose metro population was only 156,000, there were over 64,000 young men and women attending the colleges of FSU, FAMU, and TCC. Most of these students lived, worked, and played within a three mile radius of FSU campus, and during the academic year, they rarely ventured from this socially confined area unless it was to take a ten minute drive down Apalachee Parkway to get to Wal-Mart. Over 84% of FSU's undergraduate student population lived in off-campus housing which meant wherever you went in this area, you would see nothing but young people. Neighborhoods, apartment complexes, traffic stop lights, grocery stores, tanning salons, restaurants, bars, gyms, and shopping malls were all infested with college students eager to act and interact within this dynamic social community.

FSU was consistently ranked among the top party schools in the nation, but this quantitative measurement could in no way capture the true social forces at work within

Tallahassee's stimulating atmosphere of football games, pool parties, Greek socials, nightclubs, and fitness centers. The sunny Florida weather encouraged students to spend a great deal of time outdoors which made Tallahassee far more social than other college towns. Whether it was pickup basketball games at apartment complexes, Friday afternoon happy hour at POTBELLY'S, or keg parties in the backyards of student homes, students were always eager to participate in social activities that were visibly open to the public and filled with young people who wanted to have a good time. This was particularly true of football games and tailgating which were a huge part of campus life.

The Seminoles were always in serious competition for the BCS national championship and this was a powerful magnet for volatile social forces. Large public universities with nationally competitive football teams are notorious for being wild party schools with overwhelming social pressures. Drugs, alcohol, and promiscuous sex relations run rampant on most college campuses, but the degree of partying at renowned football party schools like FSU is far more extreme precisely because their notoriety attracts incoming students whose primary motivation for going to college is to get high, get wasted, and get laid. The peer pressure at these schools to live dangerously and party hard is so overwhelming that many students who do not want to participate in the party lifestyle are inevitably sucked into the social madness.

One of the primary reasons why Tallahassee was such an ideal laboratory to study human nature, social psychology, and moral behavior is because of the expansive social lives that so many students led in this party college town. Young men and women built huge interconnecting social networks of friends, associates, rivals, classmates, fraternity brothers, coworkers, sex partners, workout partners, and drug dealers. Enormous social lives exposed students to a wide and diverse range of new pressures, radical social norms, and competing moral values. The power and velocity of this socialization was truly unimaginable.

Another reason Tallahassee made such an excellent laboratory to study social behavior was because of how isolated this college town could be for students from the rest of the world. Tallahassee was for many young men and women an enclosed social environment that was completely self-absorbed, that is to say, nothing that transpired outside the immediate social lives of students mattered to them. Current events, High School friends, and even families became distant realities that had no real bearing on their lives other than concerns over parental financial support and the occasional hurricane warning. In this way, a college town like Tallahassee was a social bubble, and if you existed on the outside of that bubble, you ceased to exist.

The isolationist mentality was particularly true of mainstream students who were obsessed with their popularity and social status on campus. Since very little value was placed on the external world, some of these young people stayed in Tallahassee until their late twenties and even their early thirties. The student body treated popular students like local celebrities which made it all too tempting for young men and women working as bartenders and other fun jobs to grow overly comfortable with their big fish in a little pond status and lose all ambition to conquer the world beyond college.

Students who graduated or dropped out of school were also ensnared by Tallahassee's relatively low cost of living, its highly entertaining nightlife, and its exciting annual influx of thousands of new students every year. Sticking around town for an additional summer semester, one more football season, or the arrival of the next freshman class was the common rationale of young men and women who wanted to postpone their entry into the career world and delay the dreaded departure from the last playground.

The social isolation of a college town like Tallahassee

also made it very difficult for young men and women who did leave town to maintain friendships with students who lingered behind. You could reminisce about the past with these friends for only so long before shared memories lost their significance within the context of the ever-changing social affairs that students were now facing. It was not just that life continued on without you in your absence, this could be said of anywhere, but the social lives of young men and women in Tallahassee were so rapid and so intense that spending a month away was comparable to spending three months away anywhere else.

Students who decided to take a semester off from school would return to a place that was very different from the world they left behind because the machine never stopped and it never slowed down. The social lives of students were always expanding and constantly evolving. New friendships were quickly built and old friendships were often pulled apart by competing loyalties. Romantic relationships could seemingly develop and dissolve overnight. Personalities and interests rapidly morphed as individuals were pounded, day in and day out, with new experiences and new pressures. Change was one of the few constants that existed in a college town like Tallahassee.

A large party school like FSU also made an ideal social laboratory to study group behavior. Many students were members of cliques or larger collections of friends. Others belonged to social clubs that varied in diversity from leftwing protest organizations to the Golden Girls dance team. Greek Life was also a powerful force of socialization on campus. There were over forty fraternities and sororities at FSU, many of which boasted more than a hundred and fifty members apiece. All of these groups influenced their members with various forms of internal pressures. Dissent was punishable by harassment or even banishment and conformity often meant participating in harmful activities like discrimination, hazing, and violence.

Social clubs and Greek organizations were an important part of many students' lives, but groups like these were really just a small part of the much larger mainstream social scene. With its crowded gyms, South Beach styled nightclubs, and its more traditional bars and keg parties, the college town of Tallahassee boasted a fast-paced materialistic culture of social stratification in which who you knew, where you worked, and what you looked like determined your social status. In the Who's Who World of *The Scene*, nearly everyone was an actor putting on a show in a calculated effort to move up the ranks of the social hierarchy.

Many sacrifices had to be made by students within the mainstream college crowd because the higher someone ascended in status and the closer they moved to the center of *The Scene*, the less he or she was able to maintain their unique identity or adhere to their personal set of values. True friendships were often replaced by fake relationships between students built on their commensurate social status valuations of attraction, popularity, and prestige. To increase their social status, normative ethical standards were frequently abandoned by students in order to advance the interest of the self and group associations, often at the expense of friends and outsiders. *The Scene* had no mercy for good men because it was a cutthroat competitive environment of elitism where manipulation, intimidation, and sexual conquest were the tools of prosperity. For a way of life that revolved so much around beauty, it was all a very ugly way to live.

Once you were sucked into *The Scene*, there was no escaping its pressures. Everywhere a college student went in Tallahassee was a hypercritical social atmosphere in which you could expect to interact with numerous friends, rivals, acquaintances, and countless members of the opposite sex you wanted to impress. The exclusionary laws of social status operated fiercely within this subculture because, one way or another, students who were a part of *The Scene* were always measuring each other and ascribing to them a particular social value. Going to Strozier Library during Exam Week was nicknamed Club Strozier because the second and third floor study rooms were always overflowing with Greeks and popular students who spent more time gossiping and people watching than they did hitting the books. Skipping class on a Wednesday afternoon to lay out at the Boardwalk pool always promised a large gathering of oiled up, attractive bodies on display where many students had already started their pre-partying for tonight or were still partying from the night before. Walk across campus and you were likely to hear the clicking noise of stylish young women wearing high heels to class. A trip to the local grocery store Publix was really a trip to Club Publix where you had a better chance of picking up a member of the opposite sex than you did of remembering everything on the grocery list you forgot to bring. It is noteworthy that this particular Publix was once named by *Playboy* to be the best place in America to pick-up a hot date.

Perhaps the most competitive social atmosphere on campus could be found in the Leach Center. FSU's enormous state of the art fitness center was truly the recess playground for young adults. A trip to the gym was the ultimate "see and be seen" environment in which many students spent as much time strutting their stuff as they did exercising. Looking good was such a priority that some guys rubbed baby oil on their arms and legs to enhance their muscular definition and some girls put on makeup to sociably meander around the gym floor and pretend to workout by splashing water on their bodies in the bathroom. It was this kind of mentality that ruled the mainstream students of Tallahassee. Anywhere and everywhere you went was a part of *The Scene* where what you looked like and who you associated with determined your social status.

The status mentality of mainstream students was

exemplified by the great effort they made to enhance their appearance. Young men and women always dressed for the occasion in fashionable nightclub attire, trendy gym outfits, expensive name brand handbags, and Greek t-shirts that reflected a caste-ridden culture. Tanning salons were frequented year round and local gyms were filled with young people who exercised nearly every day, sometimes even multiple times a day. Physical vanity was the greatest sin of mainstream students and it was a vice of both the sexes.

Many college towns exert social pressure on young women to be thin, especially within Greek Life, but the level of stress endured by FSU girls to be skinny was far greater than most universities. Denied the luxury of bulky winter clothing to conceal their bodies, the college girls of Tallahassee were never able to escape the social status judgments of their peers within *The Scene* who measured the value of women almost entirely by their level of physical attraction. They thus faced overwhelming pressure to be thin, and since so many young women were in prime physical condition, there was an intense degree of social stigma felt by girls who were even slightly overweight. Eating disorders of bulimia and anorexia were very common, even among the girls who spent many hours in the gym every week. Puking to stay thin was so prevalent at FSU that the septic tanks of sorority houses were cleaned regularly and some young women learned to vomit in the showers because this reduced the likelihood that their retching would be overheard by gossiping sisters. Diet pills and illegal products like clenbuterol were also abused by young women to burn off the fat and being skinny was such a priority that some girls snorted substances like cocaine and Adderall to lose weight.

If anorexia and bulimia were common among female students, no less common was bigorexia among males who were psychologically conditioned to believe that bigger was always better. The gyms were all packed with meatheads who in their never ending quest to build more muscle would workout for excessive hours at a time and take hundreds of dollars worth of bodybuilding supplements and steroids. It might be popular for young men attending other colleges to bulk up for Spring Break with steroids, but Tallahassee's warm and sunny climate perpetuated a relentless desire among students to always look good for the beach. Steroid cycles were conducted throughout the entire calendar year and some young men never got off the juice for more than a few weeks at a time. The side-effects of mixing steroids with a party lifestyle were experienced by those unfortunate students who suffered liver damage or saw blood in their urine. A few young men even developed testicular cancer. Risks like these were worth taking because being big and getting ripped were all that mattered.

Students of *The Scene* were obsessed by their desire to have the perfect body, but it was a demanding goal achieved by many young men and women. FSU produced some of the most impressive student bodies in the United States. Weekly pool parties occurring at Tallahassee apartment complexes were spectacular events with hundreds of oiled up, toned up, ripped physiques that would have put any MTV Spring Break special to shame. The success of students who built perfect bodies raised the bar of attraction and motivated other students to strive for physical excellence. Looking your best was not always synonymous with healthy living which meant students had to be willing to pursue whatever means possible to match the difficult goal achieved by their peers.

The competition for beauty was no less demanding. Tallahassee was oversaturated with gorgeous women and this significantly reduced the unique social value of many of the female students who attended FSU. In their hometowns, pretty girls might have stuck out like a flower among the weeds, but within the FSU Greek community and the mainstream college crowd, many of these hometown beauties were just another attractive girl in a garden full of young women who were prettier, thinner, and more popular than she was. This could be a traumatic experience for a girl whose ego had been constantly bolstered in her former life by the praise and adulation of guys impressed by her good looks. No longer the center of fawning attention, these average beauties were forced to endure the stigma of being ordinary which often generated doubt of their self-worth. To make matters worse, the competition for beauty was drastically intensified by the impact of South Florida's materialistic culture.

There was plenty of natural beauty to be found among the women of Tallahassee, but there was also plenty of plastic. This was particularly true of South Florida girls from affluent backgrounds who did everything financially possible to maximize their looks. They wore color contacts, highlighted their hair and had it chemically straightened, dressed in designer clothing, adorned themselves with expensive jewelry from Tiffany & Co., went to tanning salons, had weekly pedicures and manicures, groomed their body hair with professional wax jobs, and they even had plastic surgery for liposuction. The plastic surgery fad was so popular at FSU that it was not unordinary for an eighteen-year-old girl to return to school from Winter Break with a brand new boob job. Young women who could not convince their daddies to buy them breast implants often took out additional student loans to pay for these surgical operations themselves. Nose jobs too were popular among FSU girls who were more than willing to go under the knife to achieve the flawless beauty they so desperately craved.

Plastic beauty was everywhere in Tallahassee, but the young men of this vain and self-absorbed college town did not seem to mind. Indoctrinated by the materialistic culture of South Florida and subjected to the dual influences of Hollywood and porno, most young men were enamored with plastic beauty, and in some cases, even preferred it to the real thing. Many male students, for instance, thought that silicone enhancement looked better than natural breasts. But it was not just the plastic beauty that guys liked—it was the dedication to beauty demonstrated by the young women of Tallahassee's mainstream college crowd.

Beauty sensitive females took incredibly good care of themselves. Walk into her bathroom and you would see countless bottles of expensive lotions and various feminine products used by women to pamper themselves. Open her closet and you would see more pairs of shoes than you could possibly count. Look at her naked body and it was always completely shaven of body hair. Sit next to her in your 8 AM class and she would likely have woken forty-five minutes earlier than you did that morning so that she could put on makeup and style her hair. It is undeniable that women who take care of themselves will always look better than those who do not.

The young women of Tallahassee were not alone in this meticulous grooming behavior. Whether it was going to tanning salons, highlighting their hair, or shaving their body hair, guys too were very much practitioners of plastic beauty. Some of these young men cared so much about how they looked that they shaved the hair off their fingers every day, had their eyebrows professionally waxed, and even wore tanning makeup. It was also not unorthodox for a male student to have a nose job or some other form of elective surgery to improve the way he looked. In addition to the multitude of young men who were highly self-conscious about their physical appearance, there were also many metrosexuals who knew more about fashion than their female peers. Tallahassee was swarming with trendy young men who wore designer jeans, designer shirts, and chic sunglasses that cost hundreds of dollars.

One of the primary reasons social status and physical appearance were so important to these students is because they were seeking validation of the self through respect from others. This psychological motivation was compounded by the biological reality that most college students have reached sexual maturity and are interested in exploring sexuality with desirable partners which requires that they themselves become desirable. Consequently, students who enhanced their physical appearance and aggrandized social status were more likely to maximize their sexual desires through the attraction of higher quantity and greater quality mates. College may also be perceived by students as the final time in their lives to be young and beautiful before losing their luster to the wrinkles of age, the stress of careers, and the time consuming responsibilities of family life. For all these reasons, college students within the mainstream college crowd were highly sensitive to the judgmental perception of others and went to great lengths to enhance their physical appearances and build their social reputations.

It would be a mistake to ignore the utility of social reputation and assume that the pursuit of status was purely about self-validation and sexual gratification. Whether it is through attraction, intimidation, or popularity, any form of status achieved is a form of power attained. Students who built prominent social reputations in Tallahassee were the recipients of a multitude of perks and rewards denied to their peers. A young man of status was likely to receive VIP treatment at nightclubs and bars where he was permitted to skip entry lines, drink for free, and given access into private areas of the establishment. Young women with esteemed reputations were invited to more parties and more social functions than their peers. Popular students were able to attract better-looking members of the opposite sex and they were also shown a higher degree of deference from members of their own sex. In other words, status was a social tool that played a strong hand in determining what you were able to achieve within *The Scene*. Young men and women strived to build their social reputations so that they could wield this potent means of power.

Tallahassee was truly was an ideal laboratory to live the great social experiment that is the college experience. It was a competitive college town where students isolated themselves from the external world and focused their attention completely on their status within *The Scene*. Enormous social lives exposed young men and women to a wide and diverse range of new pressures, radical social norms, and opposing moral values. Some students were able to withstand these pressures, but many were sucked into *The Scene* where they learned that manipulation, intimidation, and sexual conquest were the tools of prosperity. For a way of life that revolved so much around beauty, it was an ugly place indeed. But what better place to learn about man the social creature that he is? What better place to learn about what it took to rise to the top? And what better place to learn how strong you were at your lowest? Florida State University may not have been an Ivy League school, but what I learned socially from living in a college town like Tallahassee, I doubt very few universities could have matched.

CHARACTER KEY

Alex – Upsilon, spring pledge. Roommates with Taylor. Tall, broad-shouldered, handsome young man with freckles and auburn hair that he wore in a short buzz-cut. Tough as nails. Dark, brooding type with a lot of anger buried inside him.

Backstreet – Upsilon, younger brother. COURSE 701, bartender. Fall roommate with me and Blake. Good-looking blonde-haired South Floridian with a rough, sandpaper-faced complexion. Looked like an angry boy band member from the wrong side of the tracks. Confidently cool kid with bad boy charm.

Big Country – Upsilon, fall pledge. Big, tall, baby-faced young man from a small town in Georgia whose southern charm swooned women.

Big E - Upsilon, younger brother, Tom's big brother. Tall and lanky brother who tried to hide his premature balding by shaving his head which had the adverse effect of bringing attention to his huge ears. Aggressive with the way he hit on women.

Bill – Upsilon, older brother, part of the redneck clique. Dark-haired, burly young man from Alabama who liked to drink and liked to fight.

Bishop – Upsilon, older brother, president. Roommates with Lewis. Medium height and build with brown eyes and dark brown hair that he wore in a short, conservative hair-cut. Usually had the facial hair of a five o'clock shadow. Fervent Christian and a natural pacifist.

Blake – 706 Crew. Upsilon, younger brother. Fall roommate with me and Backstreet. Spring roommate with me and Joey. My former suitemate from the dorms. Handsome young man of Latino descent with a short muscular frame, wildly-spiky dark hair, fierce black eyes, and a ferocious temper. Bone loyal. Not a drop of fakeness in his blood.

Borelli – Upsilon, older brother, Blake's big brother. Short, muscular Italian who was into the rave scene.

Carlo – Upsilon, younger brother. Drug dealing kid from Miami. We called him the Doctor.

Clayton – Upsilon, older brother, part of the redneck clique.

Cortez – Tough Cuban from Miami who liked to play the drums and liked to fight.

Dave – Upsilon, older brother. Good-looking, pretty boy Floridian with an urban edge. Thin athletic build, blonde spiky hair worn in a tight fade, and small silver hoop earrings in both his ears.

Dickey – Upsilon, fall pledge. Was blackballed very early in the fall semester.

Fangs – Upsilon, younger brother. Short, brown-haired young man with vampire-looking teeth. Political science major who spent much of his free time doing intern work for the Governor.

Franco – Upsilon. A younger brother who failed out of school freshman year and moved back home.

Fish – Upsilon, younger brother. Roommates with Mitchell.

Well-mannered young man with auburn-brown hair, blue eyes, and an attractive face lightly speckled with freckles.

Glenn – Upsilon, older brother, part of the redneck crew. Goofy kid with glasses and crooked teeth. Liked to believe he was a leader in the fraternity.

Goldman – Upsilon, fall pledge. Red-haired, freckle-faced, quirky kid with very awkward social skills. Disliked by many of my fraternity brothers.

Horton – Upsilon, spring pledge. Floppy-haired young man with a slightly overweight build. High School buddy of Pruitt. Recruited by the redneck clique.

Jacob – Upsilon, younger brother. Roommates with Rowdy. Tall, red-haired young man renowned for speaking his mind. Also known for being a drunk.

Jake – Upsilon, younger brother. Annoying kid from California who hung out with the redneck older brothers.

Joey – Upsilon, older brother. Spring roommate with Blake, me, and his older brother Danny in the Upsilon House. Skinny, baby-faced, bashful kid with short brown hair.

Klein – 706 Crew. Upsilon, younger brother. Roommates with Moody. Handsome kid from Miami with brown hair, brown eyes, and a tall, athletically-lean build. Had a rugged metrosexual fashion sense and was the poorest Jewish kid from South Florida I ever met.

Kevin – Large black orthopedic technician.

Kronic – Upsilon, older brother, my big brother. Good-looking kid with a shaved head that he usually covered with his Cleveland Indians ball cap. Smoked a lot of weed.

Lewis – Upsilon, older brother, vice-president. Roommates with Bishop. A short-little-man whom I usually respected.

Lugar – Blake's freshman year roommate in Salley Hall. A prick we bullied into moving out.

Luke – Upsilon, spring pledge. Roommates with Tom. Handsome, muscular young man with dark hair that he wore in a short fade. Devoted Christian.

Mad Dogg – My freshman year roommate in the dorms.

McMillan – Upsilon, older brother. Square-faced, blonde-haired, hulking figure with one of those middle linebacker pair of traps that made it look like he had no neck.

Mendez – Chubby-faced Latino meathead from Ft. Lauderdale with dark hair he wore in a buzz cut. Cocky, but definitely a cool kid.

Mitchell – Upsilon, younger brother. Handsome, 6ft tall young man with light-brown hair he wore in a fade. Had long sideburns, a pointed chin goatee, and a thin muscular frame. Black belt in Taekwondo. Wanted to be a cop. Frequently played the role of a guardian angel who bailed me out of many jams. The most loyal young man I have ever met.

Moody – 706 Crew. Upsilon, younger brother, my little brother. Roommates with Klein. Handsome young man with brown hair, blue eyes, and an athletic build. Extremely competitive personality when it came to sports. A good kid you could always count on to do the right thing.

Patterson – Upsilon, spring pledge. Born and raised in Nebraska. Was one of those blonde-haired, corn-fed, naturally big and husky guys. Not the brightest kid around.

Pebbles – Upsilon, fall pledge. Short-and stocky, round-faced young man who lacked leadership qualities and social charisma. Earned the nickname Pebbles from Mitchell who believed the kid to be the only person he had ever met dumber than a brother we called Rocks, who was supposedly as "dumb as rocks."

Preston – Upsilon, older brother. Brainiac, bird-chested kid.

Pruitt – Upsilon, younger brother. Member of the redneck clique.

Raul – Upsilon, fall pledge, Blake's little brother. Big Latino from Miami who was liked by most of the brothers.

Rivera – Upsilon, younger brother. If you hadn't seen him in awhile, it was probably because he was up his girlfriend's ass.

Rocks – Upsilon, younger brother.

Rowdy – Upsilon, younger brother. Roommates with Jacob. Stood just under 6ft. tall with a muscular build. Had an eyebrow ring, blondish red hair styled in a crew-cut, and a goatee of the same color. Looked and acted like a modern day Viking. Liked to drink, liked to fight, and liked to haze.

Russo – Upsilon, younger brother. A husky, hot-blooded Italian with a buzz-cut.

Sammy – Upsilon, spring pledge. Brown-haired, stocky

young man. Good-natured baseball player. Smoked a lot of weed and always sounded high.

Santos – Upsilon, older brother. Roommates with Dave in the apartment across the hallway from me. Tall, muscular young man of Cuban descent.

Shultz – Upsilon, older brother. Tall, muscular young man with a brown-haired flat top. The best athlete in the fraternity.

Taylor – Upsilon, spring pledge, pledge class president. Roommates with Alex. Good-looking, tall, athletically-built young man with a large frame. Had a jolly personality and was an all-around good kid. Devote Catholic.

Thorne – Upsilon, older brother, part of the redneck clique. Six feet tall and athletically-built with dark eyes and dark buzz-cut hair. Could be a real asshole when he wanted to be which was quite often.

Timmy – Upsilon, fall pledge. Short squirt of a man standing at barely five feet tall. Sometimes wore glasses.

Tom – Upsilon, spring pledge. Roommates with Luke. Good-looking, muscular young man standing nearly six feet tall with crew-cut blond hair and a fair skin complexion.

Made in the USA
Lexington, KY
19 April 2015